SHATTERING
the myth of race
■
GENETIC REALITIES
AND BIBLICAL TRUTHS

Dave Unander, Ph.D.

Judson Press
Valley Forge

SHATTERING THE MYTH OF RACE
Genetic Realities and Biblical Truths

© 2000 by Judson Press, Valley Forge, PA 19482–0851
All rights reserved.

Bible quotations in this volume are from HOLY BIBLE: New International Version, copyright © 1973, 1978, 1984. Used by permission of Zondervan Bible Publishers.

Epigraphs are from John Newton's "Amazing Grace."

Library of Congress Cataloging-in-Publication Data

Unander, Dave.
    Shattering the myth of race : genetic realities and Biblical truths / Dave Unander.
      p.   cm.
Includes bibliographical references.
ISBN 0–8170–1317–2 (pbk. : alk. paper)
1. Race-Religious aspects-Christianity. 2. Race-Biblical teaching. I. Title.
BT734.U53 1999
261.8'348–dc21   99–23201

Printed in the U.S.A.

07 06 05 04 03 02 01 00

10 9 8 7 6 5 4 3 2 1

To Joe, Gina, Erica, and Tony—
may they know and live God's Word
to their generation

and to

Tony Danhelka and Dave Swinehart,
who prayed I would find my calling in life
and affirmed me in my earliest efforts at teaching.

CONTENTS

———■———

FOREWORD

—■—

I MET DAVE UNANDER IN 1976 WHEN HE WAS AN UNDERGRADUATE agriculture major. Although he was from the city of Chicago, he spent the summer working for us in Jackson and on the Voice of Calvary farm in Mendenhall, Mississippi. He was supervised by Mr. R. A. Buckley, a working farmer who was often amused by how little a college-educated agriculture student knew. Dave's former youth pastor, Tony Danhelka, had been impressed during prayer that Dave should consider working at Voice of Calvary, and, almost at the last minute, the circumstances permitted him to come.

The summer of 1976 was significant to us at the Voice of Calvary, as we were making the transition of turning the leadership in Mendenhall over to two young men whom I had discipled, Artis Fletcher and Dolphus Weary. That summer was also significant to Dave, as he met his future wife, Christine Travaglini, who had come to work for the summer in Mendenhall with a team from Bellfield Presbyterian in Pittsburgh, Pennsylvania. I had met her on an elevator at a conference in Pittsburgh, and Tom Skinner and I had encouraged her to come work with us. Thus, I played an important part in bringing Dave and Chris together! They married a year later in 1977 and now have four children, three of whom are currently in college.

For many years since, Dave and I have not seen each other. He and Chris lived in Puerto Rico for a time and are now in the Philadelphia area, while my family and I moved to California and then back to Mississippi. It is the joy of my life to cross paths again with those whom I have influenced, who are going on with the Lord and carrying on with the vision God has given us. As he relates in this book, Dave had his own set of struggles with racism from growing up in the south side of Chicago. His experiences in Chicago and Mississippi and Puerto Rico, together with the graduate studies he later did in genetics and his walk with the Lord all came together to produce this book. He hopes that it will make a unique contribution to God's kingdom, "to demolish strongholds" as Paul puts it *(2 Corinthians 10:4–5)*.

The years since 1976 have shown us that an unhealed wound from the centuries of slavery and racism still festers in America and elsewhere. Yet

God has done great things in continuing to advance the kingdom. And the words of Jesus are still true today: "If you hold to my teaching, you are really my disciples. Then you will know the truth and the truth will set you free" *(John 8:31–32)*. Today we need to hear again the liberating truth that from one blood God made the nations *(Acts 15:26)*. This book presents that truth, drawing on the evidence of the Bible, history, and the most recent genetic studies using DNA analysis. Because we need not only to reject the old lies of racism, but to produce fruit in keeping with repentance, as John the Baptist commanded *(Luke 3:8)*, *Shattering the Myth of Race* does not stop with just abstract science or theory but goes on to suggest some of the ways that our lives need to change.

John M. Perkins
John M. Perkins Foundation for Reconciliation and Development
Jackson, Mississippi

ACKNOWLEDGMENTS

■

MANY FRIENDS, COLLEAGUES, OR STUDENTS READ ALL OR PARTS of this manuscript as it has developed and often offered useful responses, questions, and suggestions. If anyone was left out of the list that follows, the oversight was not intentional. Portions of several chapters were also presented as lectures in my courses in "Genetics" or "Science, Technology and Values" at Eastern College; or as Sunday morning classes or sermons at New Life Mennonite Church, in Downingtown, Pennsylvania; or as seminars at the Instituto Cristiano de Estudios Sociales "Juan A. MacKay," Misión Integral Urbano Rural (MISIUR), in Lima, Peru; or as a faculty Bible study in the Graduate Program in Economic Development at Eastern College. The discussions and feedback in each of these settings were important and helpful, although I cannot acknowledge all the individuals involved.

In alphabetical order I would like to especially thank the following people who read through the entire book for me in one draft version or another and gave me their feedback in writing or in person. Several provided careful critiques that were especially helpful in improving the accuracy, completeness and readability. Thanks then to these readers who gave me feedback or suggestions: Nancey Coker, Nate Coleman, Nate Corbitt, Samuel Escobar-Aguirre, Lilly Escobar-Artola, Andrés Fajardo, Stephen Gatlin, Peter Genco, Allen Guelzo, K-lee Johnson, Ken and Diane Jordan, Dave Kurtz, Sonny and Eileen Lake, Robert Linthicum, Delores McCabe, Eloise Meneses, Cynthia Moultrie, John Mower, Sheldon Nix, Gowi Odera, Armando Osorio, Roz Riley, Scott and Nancy Sabin, Mark Slomka, John Stapleford, Jim Stobaugh, Nancy Thomas, Joseph Travaglini Jr., David Wilcox, and Mohan Zachariah.

My wife, Christine (Travaglini) Unander, has lived with the development of the ideas in this book for many years and also has read through parts of various versions and has given me feedback. She has also lived with my own development for many years. I owe her a great debt for her love, patience, and support throughout our marriage. Neither of us could have imagined where that single summer mission with Voice of Calvary in rural Mississippi would take us.

INTRODUCTION

—————— ■ ——————

'Twas grace that taught my heart to fear
And grace my fears relieved.

ALMOST FROM MY EARLIEST MEMORIES, THERE WAS A BACKDROP of preoccupation and sometimes conflict about race and ethnicity. As a child, this preoccupation was a source of stress and confusion to me; as an adult, I find it sometimes helps me to understand other people. Chicago in the 1960s is as good a case study as any of the manifestation of ethnic bigotry in the human heart, and the cast of characters I met there can frame the problem well. I will introduce a few of them who represent responses to ethnic strife, and I will tell you a little of my story.

REMEMBERING CHICAGO

I grew up on the far south side of Chicago, within a few miles of the city boundary. Our immediate neighborhood was mostly working-class families. Within a few blocks in one direction and a couple of miles in another were large steel mills, and the distant sound of the mammoth trip hammers used to lull me to sleep on hot summer evenings.

Few people had deep roots in the neighborhood, because much of it had been farmland until the 1920s and the 1930s or even later. In our house, English was not the only language spoken, which in our neighborhood was not unusual. From childhood through college I visited in homes in which Armenian, Dutch, German, Greek, Italian, Latvian, Polish, Spanish, or Swedish were spoken along with English. Chicago was and still is an immigrant's city. Some families had vivid stories about how poverty or war had driven them to Chicago. Some had lost all their possessions when they fled, some had suffered in prison camps, and some, among them the Armenians and the Serbs, had lost most of their families to death squads. There were also many Irish Americans, some still having bitter family memories of how they had been held back as immigrants. There had been African Americans living on the south side since before the Civil War, but my childhood fell during part of the time when many of the poorest blacks, feeling disenfranchised and angry, were coming to Chicago from the Deep South. The migration north also included many poor whites, especially from the mountains in the South, who had come trying to find work. Sometimes they were referred to as hillbillies, but not to their faces.

AN EVER-PRESENT TENSION

Although they were living in similar neighborhoods within walking distance, many blacks and whites feared and despised each other. The fruits of this attitude could be as simple as hateful stares or foul epithets but were gradually escalating to uglier incidents: brawls in the high school, throwing bricks through windows, or firebombing homes. These incidents did not occur frequently, but they did occur, sometimes without warning. The unpredictable nature of the violence left everyone on edge. When I was a child, there were two street gangs operating in the area, one white and one black, both dangerous to nonmembers of any skin color. By the time I was in high school, the Nation of Islam, as well as politicized groups such as the American Nazis and the Black Panthers, were also sometimes present. On occasion the newspaper from the Nation of Islam was delivered to our house, I assume by accident, and, as a twelve- or thirteen-year-old, I could read about how the evil of the whole world was due to the "blue-eyed devil race," who, the paper seemed to imply, were not fit to live.

While I was in high school, one of the kids I grew up with was shot and killed in a black-white fight only a few blocks from my home. I remember middle-aged family men in our neighborhood arming themselves; a man in my neighborhood barbershop showing off his new handgun; a neighbor placing shotguns in reserve at strategic sites in his house. When I was about six or seven, as we brought my grandfather home from church one Sunday night, we discovered that his living room windows had been smashed, almost certainly by some of the black kids on his block, who had been sending messages in various ways that people with his color of skin were no longer welcome. I will never forget the image of him, a bent man in his eighties who still struggled to speak English through a thick accent, standing in his living room as the streetlights reflected off the glass shards spread across his old-fashioned flowered carpet.

There were mixed messages to a child. Many of the men in my neighborhood hated or feared blacks, or both. Race was a common topic when a group of men would be talking on a front porch or in the alley: What had "they" done now? From my perspective thirty-five years later, I think that three themes were commonly echoed by the white people in my neighborhood, but it is important to note that any one person may not have believed all three at the same time. First, for many, there was real fear for their families, based on the increasing incidence of random violence against any white person. Immigrant families with no prior connection to the history of slavery and racism in the United States quickly found a reason first to fear and then to hate blacks when someone in their family was targeted by skin color in some incident.

A second common theme was bitterness against whites who were liberal, suburban, wealthier, and sometimes from old American stock (i.e., not immigrants). In this case, the grievance was based on the perception that the government would seek to redress the wrongs done by white families who had been in the United States for generations to the detriment of more recent immigrant families who shared only the same skin color. Although fear and bitterness are not commendable attitudes, neither of these responses assumed necessarily that any real differences existed in the human race. Fear and bitterness, however, lend themselves easily to justifying real racism.

The third theme expressed by only some of the whites in that neighborhood was genuine racism, a belief that most blacks were distinct from and inferior to most whites. This was a debated theme. Some of the men who were Christians, including my father, started a men's Bible study in an evangelistic effort to our neighborhood. On the south side of Chicago in the late 1960s, however, it was difficult to keep a group of invited men, some without any religion, from turning the conversation to the latest racial incident. Exiled upstairs for the evening, I would listen to the noisy arguments downstairs, as the humanity of blacks was debated.

EACH INDIVIDUAL WAS DIFFERENT

One man stood out for his anger and bitterness. He usually held down more than one low-paying job at a time, such as cleaning movie theaters. Although he had not been able to go to college, he followed technological developments closely and had a small library of books on science and history. He was proud of his atheism, relished mocking the faith of the more devout Christians in the neighborhood, and would cite H. G. Wells's Outline of History to support the triumph of science over religion. His sincere belief, argued angrily against those presenting a Christian perspective of universal brotherhood, was that science had shown the evolutionary inferiority of Africans.

This man's beliefs were hardly universal in our neighborhood. For example, one man, who was probably our only neighbor with not only a college degree but a graduate degree as well, was nationally connected in mainline church circles and directly involved in the civil rights movement. On at least one occasion, this had placed him in a shouting confrontation with Mayor Richard J. Daley, who ran Chicago as a one-party system. This man's son and I were friends, and I remember their family with affection. At times, though, there seemed to be a culture gap or inconsistencies that their neighbors wondered about. The father had little relationship with other adults in the neighborhood; he was perceived as looking down on the people who lived there and distant in the way he related to other men. Theirs was also the only house anyone knew of in our area that was cleaned regularly by a maid—a black maid. As the neighborhood became increasingly black in its demographics, this white family was one of the first to move to the suburbs, whereas some of the most verbally racist whites stayed.

I remember one such family, in which the mother had come from a poor family in the rural South and freely used racial epithets, even though she was a Pentecostal Christian. The father worked in the deepest basement of a department store in the Chicago Loop, feeding trash and discontinued merchandise into a furnace. One of their children was born with medical problems that required attention throughout his life. Occasionally during summer vacations, the mother would take a big group of us to the Lake Michigan shore in their old station wagon, in which we had to keep our feet up because of the holes in the floor. When liberal opinion leaders would make statements about the advantages and privileges of white Americans, this couple would be infuriated. They were the only people I knew who voted for George Wallace in 1968, although they realized their vote would count only as a protest. The husband had become a Christian through his wife's church, and thereafter he committed himself to regularly counseling alcoholics at a street mission in one of the skid row districts. Although they had always tended to use a lot of racial slang, they were not bothered by black neighbors and were among the last white people to move from that block, only after violence against whites in that neighborhood became inescapable. Even then, they moved only a short distance away.

AN IMMIGRANT CHURCH SEEKING TO OBEY JESUS

To travel to the Swedish Baptist church of my childhood, we would drive from our mostly white ethnic neighborhood, through a mile or so of a mostly black neighborhood, to another mostly white neighborhood. A few years before I was born, the church had made the decision to switch to English-language services. One important factor was the desire to share the gospel of Christ beyond the confines of Swedish immigrants. By the time I was a child, this working-class, Scandinavian church had attracted Italians, Greeks, Irish, Mexicans, Koreans, Russians, and various other nationalities, many of whom had risen to leadership in the church. The church was blessed with some wonderful Christian people. I remember, for example, one of my Sunday school teachers, a powerfully built steelworker with arms the size of some men's legs, who would weep openly as he spoke to his circle of little boys about the love of Jesus for us on the cross. Occasionally old hymns in Swedish would still be sung on Sunday nights. I never realized until I was an adult how humorous it could seem that some of my best friends in a Swedish Baptist Sunday school were from Italian and Mexican families.

Although there never was a barrier to southern Europeans or Hispanics or Asians in our church, a black-white wall carried over from the neighborhood into the church. I remember, for example, one man who was an electrical lineman. He was a taut, muscular man full of hair-raising tales of fixing power lines during thunderstorms. He liked to impress kids by eating whole onions like apples, and he generally came across as one tough guy. For years he had trivialized his wife's faith in Christ, but later he was dramatically converted. As he later served as an usher in our church, however, when black families came to visit, he suggested to them that they go elsewhere.

And I remember boys from a family in which the mother had come to Christ and wanted to see her sons learn about Jesus. Her oldest son was involved with a white supremacist gang and mocked any black kids who visited the Sunday school. My parents, both of whom had come to Christ in spite of situations that could have hindered their faith, also struggled with what was the right thing to do in the face of the random, violent hatred of blacks against any white person. Yet both had traveled in the Deep South and had no use for the attitudes of the whites they had encountered there. My mother, for example, had a friend who married a man in South Carolina. She had visited her friend once and remained troubled ever after by how the husband's family treated the black people in their community. She was especially surprised by the laziness: the whites did little work for themselves, not even permitting guests to help clear the table—all the labor was expected to be done by black servants.

Mature, godly Christians in the Swedish Baptist church were grieved by the racial barrier in Chicago. The senior pastor, a Swedish man from Minnesota named Bob Brunco, was wise and discerning, and he gently confronted the church with the need to take the next step of obedience to Christ, as big as switching languages, to welcoming people of all colors of skin. He succeeded—and as the neighborhood changed, the church carried on its calling, today with a mostly black congregation and a black pastor, but still with some of the original Swedes attending. As Chicago continues to be an ever-changing ethnic kaleidoscope, that congregation may have to decide if it will cross an ethnic Rubicon and reach out to the many new Asian immigrants coming into the south side.

GOD WORKS CHANGE BY HIS WORD AND HIS SPIRIT

Bob Brunco once invited a Jewish man who was a Christian and a Bible teacher to preach on racial issues. This man, Richard Wolf, had a perspective that included hiding from the Nazis in Europe as a teenager. He systematically built the biblical case of why all forms of racism and bigotry are wrong; why American racism, in particular, is wrong in God's eyes. His message was scriptural; it conveyed the spirit and the letter of Bible, and I was intellectually convinced. But even though I was only a teenager, I was developing into a fairly bitter person, and racial hatred was a root of that bitterness.

A few years later, in 1971, I was at a Christian rock festival in the Chicago Loop, in celebration of the acquittal of some rather radical Christians who had been arrested on trumped-up charges for street witnessing in front of an establishment alleged to be owned by a criminal organization. At one point during this festival, there was an invitation for prayer, especially for the baptism of the Holy Spirit. (This was a fairly Pentecostal or charismatic gathering.) This wasn't my taste in theology at that time, but I felt compelled to go forward for prayer; compelled, I believe, by the Spirit of God. I didn't have a classic Pentecostal experience. Rather than speaking in tongues or speaking at all, it was as though I was struck dumb, even in that internal monologue we all leave running. It seemed as though I witnessed in an instant a whole series of ugly things that I had committed against others, many of them involving some sort of racial hatred.

I had long trivialized or rationalized these acts, since from time to time I, too, had been a victim of violence for having the wrong color of skin. But this video playback came at the same time I was experiencing a powerful sense of the immediate presence of God, and these acts did not seem trivial or justifiable before God. There was no escape from the holiness of God that I felt. I was horrified and ashamed. It was an unforgettable moment of seeing my real self at its worst, as God had seen me all along. At that same moment, I had an overwhelming experience of the love of God in Christ for me, in spite of these evils, even as I was truly repenting. For a long time I sat weeping in a corner.

I know better than anyone how many times I have stumbled since in showing a truly Christlike character, but a foundational change had been accomplished through the Scripture and through the Holy Spirit. These alone are the agents that God has promised us will work lasting change in the human heart.

By 1984 I had gone through college and graduate studies in genetics. At that time I was living in Puerto Rico and involved in agricultural research for the University of Puerto Rico. While the Caribbean does not lack its own set of social problems, it was readily apparent that many of the racial tensions common in the United States are irrelevant there. Separating most extended families in Puerto Rico or other Caribbean islands into neat racial categories is impossible. In this setting I was talking with Jorge Dario, a pastor I know in the town of Isabela. During our discussion he made some comments concerning how 1 Corinthians 15 presents the world as being, in one sense, only two men: all humanity is either in Adam or in Christ. It was a moment of insight from the Bible, and I suddenly realized how profoundly God's Word is the foundation for destroying racism. As I further thought about this, I began to wonder where we had acquired the idea of race and whether there is any biological reality to it. This book has resulted from studying those questions.

CHAPTER I

━━━━━━━━ ■ ━━━━━━━━

Changing the Script

WHY A NEW BOOK ADDRESSING THE ISSUE OF RACE? FROM MY experience, and probably from yours also, racial identity has been such an established part of culture in the United States and many other countries that it can't be ignored. During times of social strife, race has sometimes dwarfed all other issues. Many people are surprised, then, to learn that the idea of three or four races of humanity is a relatively new one in history, and not an established fact, like the tides or the rotation of the earth.

But are there any real differences that justify an ethnic bias, differences rooted in our nature, profound chasms existing before the development of our cultural boundaries and perhaps even directing their development? Are there biological cues that genuinely break the human race into several races or subspecies and tell us in advance how someone is going to behave and think? If there are, that is the essence of the concept of race. If there are not, are we deceiving ourselves on a daily basis? In the United States, when we refer to someone in everyday conversation as "black" or "white," what does that mean? Are we talking about biology or culture?

Part of the triumph of Martin Luther King Jr.'s appeal to the conscience of Americans, black and white, was to nourish doubts about the existence of the term *race*. Since the 1960s, for many people in our country, the old racist framework has been rejected, but language to replace the old terms has not yet arisen. Steven Spielberg's 1997 film *Amistad*, taking moviegoers as close as we can go to experiencing the reality of a slave ship, has also aided the nation by giving us all a vivid insight into how the idea of race began in this country. As time moves on, new chapters in this story will be written: their content rests with us.

THE DECEPTIVE DRAMA

The central idea of this book, as the title states, is that race is a myth. There is only the human race, from every perspective: biological, historical, and in God's Word, the Bible. For the past five hundred years, Western society has been playing out a role in a drama written by the Enemy of our souls, the myth of the master race, and every act has been a tragedy. It's time to change the script.

Although politics in the United States does not today involve open campaign calls for segregation, such as commonly occurred in the American South, our culture continues to simmer with racial tensions, perhaps more openly now than in the past as expectations for the country have been raised.

Dinesh D'Souza devotes a chapter of *The End of Racism* to current episodes of bigotry and related brutality in the United States (D'Souza, 387–429). Ugly incidents originating in bigotry continue to plague us as a nation; violence of all types, often drug- or gang-related, occurs daily, and it's hard to sort out motivations after the fact. Often skin color or a different face is excuse enough: blacks and whites brawl outside a bar; a black family's home is destroyed by whites; a white college student is badly beaten by blacks; a Korean store owner is intimidated; a crowd chases teenage Puerto Ricans; and on and on. In Philadelphia, one incident in 1997 in a predominantly white neighborhood led the Roman Catholic cardinal, Anthony Bevilacqua, to write a pastoral letter to all the area's Catholics regarding the sin of racism (Bevilacqua). The country was sickened by the kidnapping of a black man and his brutal death at the hands of white supremacists in Texas in June 1998. There is evidence from the trial of Timothy McVeigh, the man sentenced for the bombing of the federal building in Oklahoma City, that he was following the ideas in a white supremacist novel, hoping to provoke a civil war along racial lines.

In our recent past are the reminders of regimes built around a racial or an ethnic identity. In June 1998, for example, a South African scientist, Daan Goosen, described for the South African Commission on Truth and Reconciliation how a secret bacterial warfare lab under the apartheid system had tried to find or develop disease strains or vaccines that would selectively kill or sterilize people with dark skins (PBS).

In the late 1990s, some Americans still hold elaborate racial myths. For example, some members of white militias hold the idea of Kingdom Identity or Christian Identity, which says that Adam and Eve were the first white people, a separate and superior species from "beasts of the field," defined as Africans and Asians (Abanes, 162–63; Kingdom Identity website). In this theology Jews are the offspring of sex between Eve and Satan (Abanes, 162; Kingdom Identity website). The motivation for a number of mass murders in the late 1990s has been connected to Kingdom Identity theology (Lessner).

The reverse of this view has been shown by the Nation of Islam, whose founder, Elijah Muhammad, preached that "the original man, Allah, is none other than the black man. The black man is the first and last, maker and owner of the universe. . . . The white race is not, and never will be, the chosen people of God" (quoted in D'Souza, 427). In this theology, all nonblack peoples were bred from the original blacks by an evil scientist, Yacub, with whites being the last and most dangerous. Exiled to Europe, whites allegedly mated with animals, thus producing the Jews.

A common theme in these racial theologies is hatred of the Jews, a hatred that suggests the hidden, demonic origin of these theologies.

A WAY OF SEEING THE WORLD

By the time you have finished this book, I hope that if you currently believe that the world is divided into races, you will do so no longer, and if you do not but aren't sure why you don't, this book will help supply a reason for your conviction. My prayer for this book is that God can use it to "prepare God's people for works of service, so that the body of Christ may be built up until we all reach unity in the faith and in the knowledge of the Son of God and become mature, attaining to the whole measure of the fullness of Christ" (Ephesians 4:12–13).

In recent decades, there has been a great deal of shame in the United States over the racist parts of our history, and one outcome of this has been for many whites to ignore the past, even the recent past, and the effects centuries of bigotry have had on a shared way of thinking. For example, during my childhood, restaurants, movie theaters, buses, and even drinking fountains in many states still maintained openly, and with the full force of the law, separate facilities for anyone with even a portion of African ancestry. To most of us today, this sounds like conditions in Nazi Germany, when signs were posted restricting or isolating Jewish Germans from the rest of their society. This, however, was a system maintained not by a police state

3

but by a people committed to democracy, by people who were often otherwise decent yet truly believed that African ancestry, even a small amount, made a person belong to a different and lower category of humanity, perhaps not even human. Black Christian writers such as Tony Evans or Jefferson Edwards identify the need to take apart this myth that has affected all of us. Although we may be ashamed of events long past as well as the recent past, we have to face up to it to move on.

We can see one example of how short the history of this change of perspective is when we consider science fiction plots from Hollywood. In 1966 the casting of Nichelle Nicols as Lieutenant Uhura on the original *Star Trek* was considered daring for American television, although she was virtually the only black crew member ever seen on this ship of the twenty-third century. For the first year of the show she was also the only cast member without a contract (Infusino, 56).

In contrast, in 1993 *Star Trek: Deep Space Nine* premiered with Avery Brooks, an African American, in the role of commander of a troubled space station in the twenty-fourth century, attempting to broker peace following a situation in which there had been generations of oppression of one people by another. If ever science fiction could be seen as a barometer of its time, this was it. In one of the most powerful episodes, "Far Beyond the Stars," Brooks was yanked back to New York City in the 1950s, where he found himself working as a science fiction writer for a pulp magazine. The plot developed around his struggle to get a white publisher or fellow writers—and even other African Americans in Harlem—to accept the *Deep Space Nine* plot, especially the idea of a black space commander.

Although there are many excellent books on particular aspects of this topic, I am not aware of any one book that pulls together insights from history and genetics with the truth of the Bible. I write from an evangelical Christian perspective, and I will make a case that the Bible presents the revelation of God and Jesus Christ that we need to rise above our natural inclination toward division and violence. This book is not intended to be exhaustive in any of these areas. My desire is that this book will give a Christian perspective fitting together understanding from diverse disciplines into a coherent whole and will help to change ways of thinking but also ways of feeling. I know that it is impossible to fully incorporate all the research ongoing in genetics, but I believe a sound understanding of the emerging scientific picture concerning human genetic diversity based on research from the last twenty years is possible. I hope this will not be the last book you read on the topic of races but rather that it proves to be a good source for further reading or for reference.

INSIGHTS FROM HISTORY

One could say there were no races before 1400, because the concept of race as it is commonly used in our time did not exist. Or, if it did exist, the idea occurred mainly among Muslim Arab slavetraders, who during the Middle Ages seem to have developed a theology of African inferiority. By the 1400s, through Spanish and Portuguese contact with Arab slavetraders in Africa, the institution of slavery was returning to Europe. The need to justify slavery to a Christian culture first opened the door to the concept that Africans were a different type of people, intended by nature to serve others.

By the 1500s the Spanish were wrestling with the question of the origin of the Native Americans and their human rights under both church and royal law. The enormous plunder and profits at hand for the *conquistadores* spawned the theology that the Native Americans were a different kind of human, perhaps not even descended from Adam, and not subject to the same legal protection. This was quickly extended to include the Africans being brought as slaves to replace the Native Americans who were dying from Old World diseases. As the slave trade and colonial empire building spread among the European countries, so also seems to have spread the concept of races, which were generally perceived as being four: black, red, white, and yellow, corresponding to the peoples originally of Africa, the Americas, Europe and the Middle East, and East Asia. Where the boundaries among these races were to be drawn was a problem that racists have never resolved.

As a skeptical approach to the Bible became increasingly popular during the Enlightenment, the scriptural teaching of the common origin of humanity was widely rejected, and scientific support for racial differences was claimed. For example, humanity was broken into four distinct species by Linneaus, the originator of scientific taxonomy. The idea of races fit well with the mystical idea of the Great Chain of Being that was popular among European academics, particularly if white Europeans were placed in some type of leadership caste. Races were also easily incorporated into evolutionary theory.

5

But where did the boundaries lie? At various times, skin color, skull volume, skull shape, and, finally, test scores such as the intelligence quotient (IQ), were proposed as demonstrating clear racial differences, with the white race believed to be superior, higher on a mystical Chain of Being or better fit to rule by evolutionary selection. This remained the prevailing perspective among many scientists and policy makers associated with major universities and government institutions through World War II, when Nazi Germany provoked a moral revulsion against these ideas taken to a logical conclusion.

Not everyone was silent about the idea of race and the exploitation it justified. For example, Bartolomé de las Casas was a Dominican priest, sent to the Americas in the 1500s, who made his life's work developing a Christian case against the concept of races. Although he was only partly successful in seeing his academic battles result in sweeping social changes, today his memory is honored in many Latin American countries for the lives he did save and the foundation he laid for the end of slavery. In the 1700s John Woolman was a Quaker evangelist from New Jersey who likewise devoted a large portion of his effort against slavery and the concepts behind it. Eventually the Quakers became the first Christian denomination to break with the institution of slavery since its return to Europe, and Woolman was one of the influences in this change. We will also draw from examples of contemporary Christians seeking to be peacemakers.

INSIGHTS FROM GENETICS

My graduate training was in genetics, the scientific study of how heredity works. To discuss the way science was used to support racism, I'll review some of the basic concepts of genetics and evolution, as well as examples of how the scientific culture became associated with racism.

We now understand that characteristics passed from one generation to the next are controlled by one to many genes, each made of the molecule DNA. Some traits seem to be controlled by only a single gene, with various versions of that gene available within a species. Eye color in humans is like this—whether one has blue or brown eyes is the result of a single gene. But even eye color is not that simple: some people have green or hazel eyes; and think of the varying shades of blue or brown eyes.

Human skin colors combine varying amounts of melanin, the dark-colored molecule that accumulates as a defense response to intense sunlight (tanning); carotene, the Vitamin A precursor, stored in fat just under the skin, closer to the surface in some people, adds yellow and golden hues; and small blood vessels which in some people are closer to the surface of the skin add pink and red hues. For inherited differences in melanin, the chemical that produces skin color differences from black to white, at least five genes are involved. The "positive" form of each of these genes is believed to signal the skin to produce one more "dose" of melanin, whereas the "negative" form of the gene provides no such signal. Since we have two parents, each giving us one copy of each of those genes, there are at least eleven shades of black to white in human skin color. Since it is common to find several to many forms of a gene within a species, this model of only eleven shades is probably far too simple.

We carry an estimated eighty thousand genes, for many different kinds of traits (Human Genome Project). Only a very small number of these would be inherited consistently linked to any of the genes for melanin; that is, different shades of skin tone could not predict the other genes any individual carries. Further, the number of genetic combinations staggers the mind. Each human sperm or egg cell contains one out of more than eight million new genetic combinations of the person it came from. Since each conception is the result of two parents, each new individual is one combination out of a minimum of some eight million times eight million possibilities just for that particular mother and father. In addition, each new person then grows up with all the influences of his or her native language and culture, the personalities of the people around him or her, and the impact of any nutritional deficiencies or diseases. Attributing a simple genetic cause to predict any complex behavior or lifestyle is absurd.

This is the essential deception of racism and other types of bigotry: that some simple key will reliably predict the behavior of others. A sound realization of the many factors interacting to make a human personality should help us to realize the danger of oversimplification: attributing a human behavior to a single gene (e.g., the criminal gene or the gay gene).

In only the most recent decades has it been possible to compare populations based on DNA differences in many genes, most of which do not even produce effects visible to the eye. As we shall see from a survey of some of this work, at the level of the eighty thousand genes of humanity, there are no racial frontiers or even clear ethnic frontiers among nationalities.

Genetically, we all belong to highly smudged categories within the one human race, which, at the level of DNA, seems to reflect a geologically recent origin from a narrow population base. That is scientific terminology to say that there is good evidence to say that we are one human family, not four, fairly recently spread out across the earth.

INSIGHTS FROM THE BIBLE

As we survey the Bible, we find an absence of anything suggesting or supporting the concept of race as the term has been used in the past five hundred years. Compared with our contemporary literature, the Bible displays a remarkable lack of physical descriptions of any kind. There is a message in Scripture through what is not said.

In the Bible there has never been a rigid ethnic boundary to the people of God; the issue always has been one of faith and not of DNA. In the revelation given to the apostle John, before the throne of God there was an uncountable multitude (Revelation 7:9). These were of every ethnic group ("nation"), tribe, people, and language. This is a fascinating concept, suggesting that our cultural backgrounds will somehow still be identifiable in heaven, but as even the most extravagant achievements become irrelevant and are cast before the throne of God in worship (Revelation 4:10), they won't seem important anymore. Absent from John's revelation is any remaining identification on the basis of a human political entity or anything suggesting our word race. There are no tears in heaven—or races. Instead the Bible has much to say about the image of God in humanity and about his revelation for us. In the final chapters of the book I will discuss these, as well as reconciliation and peacemaking.

CHAPTER 2

■

Roots of the Concept
of Race

Through many dangers, toils, and snares,
We have already come.

ESTERN SOCIETY HAS AT LEAST THREE MAIN ROOTS, AS WELL AS important influences from other sources (e.g., Weatherford, for his perspective on Native American influences). We can easily identify Greek and Roman culture and philosophy; Judaism, Christianity, and the influence of the Bible; and, since the Renaissance and the Enlightenment, science and the concept of progress and industrialization. These diverse roots are one reason for the often contradictory objectives expressed by contemporary culture. Modern science has Christian roots in the Renaissance and Reformation and is committed to finding an objective, knowable truth. Thus, theoretically at least, there should be no conflict between a Christian and the findings of science. Western culture, however, has also developed among its core values industrialization and progress—the idea that change is inevitable and will always be for the better—and these have their own internal logic that has sometimes been at odds with biblical values.

THE CLASSICAL WORLD

M. T. Hodgen (1964) has reviewed concepts of humanity prior to recent centuries, and in writing this section I am indebted to her book. People are usually curious about other people, and accounts of life among people with strange customs have always been popular, whether the stories were told by Herodotus, Marco Polo, or Viking sagas. Hodgen shows, however, that until a few centuries ago there was no concept of distinct branches of the human race that would correspond to that concept in contemporary culture. For example, Pliny the Elder (A.D. 23–79) cataloged information about hundreds of ethnic groups in Europe, Africa, and Asia (e.g., "there are five German races," in Hodgen, 36), but the differences discussed by Pliny are mostly those of customs and occupations (e.g., tattooed, long-haired; shepherds, foresters). The Greeks alluded to the Egyptians being darker-skinned than they were, but the Greeks described all foreigners as "barbarians" (Lefkowitz, 13). The Roman physician Galen made reference to the Ethiopians having short hair, but his attention was drawn to their dry skin, not their dark skin (Galen, 535). Similarly, Lewis, focusing on Middle Eastern peoples, finds prejudice among classical cultures such as ancient Egypt or Sumeria but no evidence that any particular skin color carried a consistent meaning: clothing, hair, and beard styles, along with language and religion, seemed to play the major role in ethnic identification (Lewis, 17–18). Ancient Egypt would be described by contemporary Americans as a multiracial society; that is, people did not discriminate on the basis of skin color, and there was substantial variability in the appearance of Egyptians, although they viewed all non-Egyptians with disdain (Ortíz de Montellano, 35).

The ideas of Plato and Aristotle were sometimes adapted to racist ideologies and thus deserve attention in this review. Although his proposals for the ideal society seem in some ways totalitarian, Plato does not seem racist in our understanding of the term. Plato spoke of men being in quality like gold, silver, bronze, or iron, but these differences do not necessarily follow family lines, and a common humanity is acknowledged. For example,

> God differentiated those qualified to rule by mixing in gold at their birth. The auxiliaries he compounded with silver, and the craftsmen and farmers with iron and brass. So endowed, each will usually beget his own kind. . . . Nevertheless they are all related to one another; therefore it may sometimes be that a silver child will be born of a golden parent, a golden child from a silver parent and so on. . . . Should they [i.e., the golden] themselves beget sons alloyed with brass or iron, they are forbidden to take pity upon them in any way; they must assign to each one a status appropriate to his nature . . . among the farmers and craftsmen. (Plato *Republic* 3.415)

Later, Plato commands that the golden rulers not be permitted to possess their own houses or accumulate wealth (*Republic* 3.416–17). In fact, Plato condemns "idle men who live extravagantly" as being so dangerous to the republic that they should be "exterminated as quickly as possible" (*Republic* 9.564). Whatever may be the implications of Plato's ideal society, its concepts do not seem to be those that undergirded racist societies, although his ideas do sound like genetic determinism, that genetic endowment determines destiny.

Plato's younger contemporary Aristotle developed further the idea of people born inferior and wrote of "slaves by nature." He began his career as a junior associate of Plato but later became teacher to Alexander the Great and many other leaders in Greek society. As Greek culture was dispersed and promoted throughout Alexander's empire, Aristotle's books and many of his ideas were adopted by the Romans, the Jews, the Arabs, and later the Renaissance cultures, including the Spanish at the time of the *Conquista*. His concepts of nature, such as the "four humors" that he believed determine health and illness, were dropped by modern science since the 1700s but live on within Mexican, Arabic, and some Asian Indian traditional medicine. However, *Politics*, Aristotle's systematizing of political theories and national policy, remains a surprisingly contemporary and insightful book, complete in its summary of types of political options open to a society. Aristotle's natural science has been abandoned for centuries, but relatively little change has taken place in politics.

In *Politics* 1.4–5, Aristotle discusses slavery, paralleling modern management theory when he describes both employees and slaves as being animate tools as opposed to inanimate tools, placed in the hands of men wise enough to give appropriate orders (Aristotle, 10–11). The critical passage is in 8–11 of chapter 5 (Aristotle *Politics* 13–14):

> We may thus conclude that all men who differ from others as much as the body differs from the soul, or an animal from a man . . . all such are by nature slaves, and it is better for them . . . to be ruled by a master. A man is thus by nature a slave if he is capable of becoming . . . the property of another. . . . We have hitherto been speaking of mental differences. But it is nature's intent also to erect a physical difference between the body of the freeman and that of the slave, giving the latter strength for the menial

duties of life, but making the former upright in carriage. . . . The contrary of nature's intention, however, often happens: there are some slaves who have the bodies of freemen—as there are others who have a freeman's soul. . . . Just as some are by nature free, so others are by nature slaves, and for these latter the condition of slavery is both beneficial and just.

The perspective is rather pragmatic: those who have been captured and made slaves must have deserved it.

Note the qualifications that Aristotle places on his own statements, as well as the internal contradictions. First he says that those who are by nature slaves differ from other men as much as animals differ from people. How do we identify these people of a slave biology? Besides being more physically fit for working than thinking, Aristotle says, if someone has become the property of another, that demonstrates that he must have the nature of a slave. He suggests that sometimes mistakes are made, but he skips over these and concludes that those who truly are by nature slaves benefit from being managed under bondage. For later consideration of the issue of race, Aristotle noted no physical differences other than strength for hard tasks that would aid in identifying those who are "slaves by nature." No mention is made of skin color, and many slaves were prisoners of war from all parts of the world known to the Greeks.

EARLY CHRISTIANS

The Roman writer Pliny and many others, both before and after him, told stories about creatures we could perhaps best call humanoids. These included blemmies, men without heads but with eyes and mouths in their chests; satyrs, men with feet of goats; and a variety of others. That is, they were creatures with a resemblance of human form but radically different from the normal human body plan. Augustine, in *The City of God,* established the Christian standard of the early church on the idea of even such radical human diversity as satyrs or blemmies: "Either the stories of such monsters are plain lies, or if there be such, they are either not men, or if they be men, they are the progeny of Adam" (Augustine *City of God* 16.8).

A good example of the attitude of the early Christian church toward human diversity can be found in *The Call of All Nations,* by Prosper of Aquitaine, a lay teacher in the south of France and a contemporary of

Augustine. In this book, written around 450, Prosper wrestles with the problem of God's sovereignty and human will. Rather than wondering whether some peoples are born cursed by God and others born blessed, Prosper stresses again and again the common, universal state of all humanity, lacking any innate merit that would force God's hand in saving them or favoring one people above another (e.g., Prosper *The Call of All Nations* 1.6–7). Discussing Isaiah 9:2, "The people walking in darkness have seen a great light; on those living in the land of the shadow of death a light has dawned," he emphasizes that this shows how Christ came to save all who had no spiritual standing before God, which is to say, all of us (1.15). God's ultimate intention has always been for spiritual children of Abraham, not limited to a physical lineage, as expressed through Jeremiah's prophecies (Jeremiah 31:31–34) that a day would come when his laws would be written on the heart and not just on tablets of stone (1.9). Discussing the Great Commission of Jesus *(Matthew 28:18–20)*, to "go and make disciples of all nations," Prosper comments,

> *Does this command make a difference between any peoples or any individuals? No, he welcomed no one for his merits, singled out no one for his birth, made no distinction with anyone because of his social state. The gospel of the cross of Christ was extended to all men without exception. (2.2).*

ARAB ISLAMIC CULTURE AND MEDIEVAL EUROPE

Bernard Lewis, a scholar of Middle Eastern languages at Princeton University, has attempted the first major study of the concept of race in medieval Islam, published as *Race and Slavery in the Middle East*. In the earliest Islamic society, Lewis has concluded, there was relatively little ethnic bigotry among Muslims, consistent with a lack of bigotry in the Qur'an (e.g., Lewis 1990, 21), but following the conquest of North Africa (late 600s), a distinction based on skin color gradually developed (Lewis 1990,18–20).

Lewis has attempted to trace the earliest record of the concept of "the curse of Ham" being identified with a dark skin, and he may have found it in the works of a Muslim teacher. Wahb ibn Munabbih, discoursing about 828, explicitly stated that Noah was a handsome white man and God changed the color of Ham and his descendants to black in response to Noah's curse (Lewis 1990, 124–25). "These Islamic versions depart in two significant versions from the biblical and rabbinic versions: first that Ham, who is stricken by the curse, is presented primarily as the ancestor of the dark-skinned peoples; second, that the curse consists of the double burden of servitude and blackness" (Lewis 1990, 125). Blacks who converted to Islam were promised the blessing of having white skins in Paradise (Lewis 1990, 35).

In contrast to medieval Europe, in which slavery shrank to a minor part of the economy, Islamic societies continued to depend on enormous numbers of slaves, with the majority of these eventually coming from sub-Saharan Africa. Arab and Persian writers from the late Middle Ages in Europe (c. 900s and afterward) wrote of black Africans as being more similar to animals than to humans (Lewis 1990, 52–53).

The Arabs invaded Spain in 711 and continued to be present in parts of the country until 1492. One of the first results of their conquest was sale of large numbers of captured Spaniards and Goths as slaves (Appleton et al., 68–69). Because of the Arab presence, slavery remained common in Spain and Portugal while it was uncommon elsewhere in medieval Europe. Whatever concepts of the inferiority of black Africans were developing among Arabs were also culturally available to the Spanish and the Portuguese.

MEDIEVAL CHRISTIANS

The perspective of the human race as one, based on common descent from Adam, was the paradigm of all Judeo-Christian cultures through at least the 1500s, even as more and more diverse peoples were encountered during the Age of Discovery. A strong rabbinic tradition prevailed through the Middle Ages, for example, that the curse of Ham was restricted only to the children of Canaan, even if only as a legal fiction (Lewis 1990, 5, 104–5); other non-Canaanite peoples were not destined in any particular way for slavery or freedom.

> The problem of pigmentation, already a very old one at the time of the Renaissance, was stilled somewhat as an element in intergroup relations by the confident Europocentric theory that variation in complexion was ascribable to difference in length of exposure of originally white skins to the rays of the sun. The popularity of this theory helped to keep the Negro and other dark-skinned peoples theoretically in the family of Adam, thus upholding their dignity as human beings. . . . Peoples were

differentiated from one another as "nations," while the term "race" carried a zoological connotation properly applicable only to animals. As long as man—even pigmented man—was regarded as monogenetic in origin and homogeneous in descent, he could not be submitted to zoological divisions, or to the terms used to designate them. (Hodgen, 214)

As Hodgen documents at length, by the 1600s this perspective was being undermined throughout European cultures. There was a major change of perspective, a paradigm shift, from viewing the human race as one, descended from Adam, to seeing several distinct species or subspecies—"races"—with the white race clearly superior and fit to rule the others.

THE SPANISH CONQUISTA AND THE DEBATES OF LAS CASAS AND SEPÚLVEDA

Columbus died believing he had found islands somewhere in the western approach to India, inhabited, of course, by Indians. India, while exotic to Mediterranean and European peoples, was still a known land (e.g., Esther 1:1). The earliest Spanish colonists were sometimes brutal but still seemed initially to believe they were dealing with another Asian people, equally human as they were. (The Indians also had to find a category for the Spaniards. In some experiments carried out with captured *conquistadores,* the Tainos in Puerto Rico concluded the Spanish were merely other men like themselves.) Within a few decades, however, it was generally clear that a continent unknown to Europe had been found. This created a new problem of understanding how the American Indians were related to other, known peoples.

However, the curiosity about Native American origins was of little importance relative to the slow but constant pressure of *conquistadores* and colonists, steadily enslaving each new people they encountered for work in mines and plantations. Nonetheless, there were many Spaniards with a strong biblical belief in the unity of humanity, even while they were prepared to exploit the peoples they found. Even Francisco Pizarro, the conqueror of the Incas in the 1500s, issued commands setting limits on his soldiers' activities, because "the native inhabitants of this country . . . were, in God's words, created as our brothers and are descendants of our first ancestor" (Hemming, 140).

From the beginning there was a double-mindedness to the Spanish arrangement. *Conquistadores* within the law (not all were) were granted a feudal *encomienda*, literally a trust or a commission, of land and Indians to rule over, but with the proviso that the purpose of this delegated authority was to teach the gospel first and only afterward turn a profit. This was based on a papal bull entrusting to Spain the evangelism of the new lands. This proviso was often a legal fiction, but not completely, and Spanish colonists of integrity had troubled consciences. Particularly in those cases when Indians converted to Catholic Christianity, there were Spaniards concerned that they were sinning by keeping fellow Christians as slaves.

A theological solution, proposed and eventually widely accepted, was that these new peoples were different in nature and destined to be slaves, independent of their acceptance of the Christian faith. This conviction can be seen by occasions when the Spanish *conquistadores* seem to have been surprised that the Indians would rebel against them. In 1533, when the remnants of the Inca army mounted a serious challenge, Francisco Pizarro's secretary noted, apparently with astonishment, "The reason why these Indians rebelled and were seeking war with the Christians was that they saw the land being conquered by the Spaniards, and they themselves wished to govern it" (Hemming, 92).

The justification for this idea came from Aristotle, who, as we have seen, had proposed natural slavery. By the Age of Discovery, Aristotle was held in enormous respect in the Roman Catholic church. Within the construct of Thomas Aquinas, Aristotle was a bearer of God's Word through natural and systematic reason, God's parallel communication to the supernatural revelation of the Bible.

John Major, a Scottish professor in Paris, was the first person known to have applied Aristotle's passage about slaves by nature to the Native Americans, in a book published in 1510 (Hanke, 14). This new application was first opposed a year later by a Dominican priest in Hispanolia, Antonio de Montesinos (Hanke, 15; the memory of Montesinos is honored today in the Dominican republic by a huge, dramatic statue of him on the shoreline of Santo Domingo). The opposition of Montesinos led to the first policy to protect Native Americans, the Laws of Burgos. Shortly after this event, leadership of the opposition to the way the Spaniards were treating the Tainos and other Indians shifted to Bartolomé de las Casas. Las Casas's comments on Major's book includes a famous quote, "I in no way think that John Major himself would tolerate a situation so impious and brutal if he were an Indian" (Gutiérrez, 87).

Las Casas had a remarkable life, the basic facts of which are sketched in many books (e.g., Hanke; Helps; Gutiérrez). He was born in Seville in 1474, the son of a man who later sailed on Columbus's first voyage. Columbus's own log book was lost some centuries later, but a combination of transcriptions and summations made by Las Casas in the early 1500s from the original log are the main source of primary data to historians about Columbus's first voyage. Las Casas first visited the Caribbean in 1498, returned as a colonist in 1502, and was ordained as a priest in 1507.

In 1514, at the age of forty, Las Casas underwent a profound conversion experience while preparing a sermon for Pentecost. He repented of his sins in the Spanish conquest of Hispaniola and devoted his life to evangelism and justice for the Native Americans. This included pastoral service as a Dominican priest in present-day Cuba, Guatemala, and Mexico, years of lobbying and legal groundwork before the royal court in Spain and elsewhere on behalf of Native Americans, and extensive writing. He was still involved in both writing and politics at the time of his death in 1566: he was revising some of his books to the end. He was a contemporary of Columbus and the *conquistadores,* Erasmus, Luther, Calvin, Loyola, da Vinci, Michelangelo, and the Borgia popes. Although he is not well-known in the United States, a number of Latin American countries celebrate a Las Casas holiday in his honor.

In 1519, Las Casas returned to Spain to argue against the use of Aristotle's concept to justify enslaving the Native Americans, a concept that was then being promoted by the bishop of Darien, Juan Quevado (Hanke, 16). In his debate with Quevado, before Emperor Charles V, Las Casas described Aristotle as a "Gentile burning in Hell, whose doctrine we do not need to follow except in so far as it conforms with Christian truth" (Hanke, 16). Considering that Aristotle almost had canonical status in some Catholic circles at that time, this was a daring statement.

Besides being bluntly skeptical of Aristotle as an authority equal to the Bible, Las Casas began to document the achievements of the cultures of the Native American peoples beginning in 1527, in *Historia de las Indias,* which he worked on until his death. One purpose was to demonstrate that the Native Americans were fully the equals of peoples from Europe and the classical Mediterranean cultures. He also sought to document the atrocities of his own people, published in 1542 in *Brevísima relación de la destrucción de las Indias,* translated in English as *Tears of the Indians.* His motivations are expressed near the end of that book:

> I Friar Bartholmew Casaus, of the Order of St. Dominic, who went to these parts through the mercy of God, desiring the salvation of the Indians, that so many precious souls redeemed with the blood of Christ might not perish, but wishing with my whole heart, that they might through the knowledge of their Creator live eternally: Because of the care also and compassion which I bear to my country, which is Castile, fearing lest God should destroy it in his anger for the sins which it has committed against his divine Majesty . . . (Las Casas, 84)

Juan Ginés de Sepúlveda, a leading Spanish philosopher and political theoretician, built an elaborate argument, based on the writings of Aristotle, that all the Native Americans were by nature among those destined to be slaves. Part of his argument was that since they were being conquered by the Spanish, they must be inferior people. Native Americans in the present-day Mexican states of Oaxaca and Chiapas delegated Las Casas with authority to represent them, for which purpose Las Casas returned to Spain permanently in 1547 (Hanke, 29). In 1548, Sepúlveda published a major work, the first translation of Aristotle's *Politics* into Latin (Hanke, 31), the language of the intellectuals of that day. Simultaneously, Las Casas was lobbying for stricter laws protecting Native Americans, but there was sometimes violent opposition or passive neglect to obey. In Peru, for example, the first viceroy sent by the king expressly to enforce these new laws was killed by a mob of *conquistadores* (Hanke, 34). Similarly, in 1540 Charles V had ordered all African slaves in all Spanish dominions set free, but this injunction was widely ignored, and slavery gradually regained lost ground in the Spanish empire (Wesley 1774, 5). Finally, in 1550, Charles V, by then Holy Roman emperor and not just king of Spain, ordered all further conquests in the Americas to cease until a commission of theologians and counselors could weigh a debate between Sepúlveda and Las Casas regarding Aristotle's doctrine of "slaves by nature" applied to Native Americans (Hanke, 36–37).

Throughout his works and his debate with Sepúlveda, Las Casas sought to document both the complete humanity of the cultures of the Indians and the brutality of the *conquistadores* in their quest for quick riches. G. Gutiérrez notes how Las Casas stressed the urban achievements of the Native Americans, their cities, high culture, and architecture: he was not describing an idealistic noble savage contrasted with civilized Europeans, as Rousseau did, but rather a culture similar in many ways to that of Europe, with its own atrocities and its own high achievements (Gutiérrez, 299).

Sepúlveda had several arguments, including the idea that it would be easier to evangelize once the Native Americans were subjugated, as well as the argument from Aristotle that some people were by nature slaves—and these were such people (Hanke, 41). He believed them to be as different, "finally, I might almost say, as monkeys to human beings" (Gutiérrez, 293), not the last time that this analogy would emerge. In contrast, Las Casas kept returning to the Bible as his authority that humanity is alike before God: if this conflicts with Aristotle, Las Casas's exact words were "Too bad for Aristotle" (Gutiérrez, 297). Sepúlveda grouped "barbarians" fit for slavery into three groups, again after Aristotle, and placed the Native Americans in the lowest group of the three; Las Casas, arguing from the Bible, saw all humanity created in the image of God and "redeemed by the most precious blood of Christ" (Gutiérrez, 296). Like William Penn more than a century later, Las Casas documented Native American culture. Although he was committed to evangelism, he, also like Penn, held that belief could not be compelled, as it customarily was under the Spanish scheme of that time; liberty of conscience had to be part of evangelism (e.g., Gutiérrez, 208–10, 304).

There is not a consensus among historians as to how much effect Las Casas had in restraining exploitation by the *conquistadores*, but it is generally thought that in his absence, it would have been worse. The pope, for example, used Las Casas's words to condemn enslaving Native Americans in the West Indies (Gutiérrez, 307), but many of the Catholic colonists chose to ignore the pope's order (Gutiérrez, 308). A story that illustrates the real *conquistador* religion was told by Las Casas (Gutiérrez, 442):

> A certain chief summoned all of his people and ordered them each to bring their gold to one place and make a pile of it. And he told his Indians: "See, friends, this is the Christians' god. Let us dance before it a bit, and then sail out upon that sea and cast it into the waters. Once they know that we do not have their god, they will surely let us be."

Early in his career, Las Casas had proposed to free Native American slaves if they were replaced with African slaves, on a limited basis, in order to preserve the lives of the Native Americans. A few years after writing that, he repented of it and devoted additional chapters of his *History of the Indies* to documenting the evils of the African slave trade on both sides of the Atlantic (Gutiérrez, 326–29). He argued from the same scriptural basis as he did regarding Native Americans: that God has commanded a common justice to all humanity. Spanish law did establish rights lacking elsewhere for African slaves: every slave was to have a free day in addition to Sunday, in which money could be earned in independent work. The law permitted slaves to gradually purchase additional free days and eventually their freedom. No slave was a slave forever by nature (Wesley 1774, 43).

Las Casas both won and lost. At the level of Spanish policy, he succeeded in establishing some laws recognizing the legal rights of the Native Americans as human beings. In publicizing atrocities that were being hidden from much of the European public, he shamed some officials into action. Many of the Native Americans did not lose their lands in the way they did in the United States and Canada, and so native cultures and peoples in many cases survived. In addition, the extreme prejudice against mixing of nationalities did not develop as it did in North America, and this fact is partly the fruit of Las Casas and other Spaniards with a strong Christian conscience. The moral character of Las Casas and his works, and the fact that Spain at the peak of its power tried to heed what Las Casas was saying, have been cited as reflecting the best in Spanish culture (e.g., Hemming, 257). At a popular level, his heart for the oppressed won him the love and respect of millions of Latin Americans.

However, at a pragmatic level, policies to guard the rights of Native Americans or Africans were often de facto ignored: Las Casas had not succeeded in his day in morally convicting most of the slaveowners and *conquistadores*. By 1566 the first English slave ship arrived in Africa (Wesley 1774, 15). The concept of slave races now existed in the minds of men of energy and enterprise throughout Europe, men who needed only a seemingly reasonable justification before acting on their impulses of conquest and profit.

CHAPTER 3

■

Race and Economics

THE DEVELOPMENT AND REFINEMENT OF THE IDEA OF RACES OF humanity grew up with both modern science and higher criticism of the Bible. For example, by 1655 Isaac de la Peyrère, a theologian in the Low Countries, was questioning whether Moses wrote the first five books of the Bible (the Pentateuch), as well as questioning much of Genesis, specifically that the human race only had one origin (Hodgen, 273–76). In England, William Petty, a member of the Royal Society, presented and published a formal paper, "Scale of Creatures" (1676–1677), formally suggesting the existence of distinct races of man, all within a scheme modeled after the Platonic great chain of being, with levels of superiority and inferiority (Fredrickson 1981, 11; Hodgen, 408, 419–24).

Carolus Linnaeus, the Swedish botanist who invented scientific taxonomy in the 1700s, divided the human race into two species (*Homo sapiens* and *Homo monstrous;* Hodgen, 425–26). *Homo monstrous* included fantasy humanoids such as those mentioned in chapter 1. *Homo sapiens,* Latin for "wise man," was broken into five races by Linnaeus, which he defined as (Linnaeus, quoted in Hodgen):

Wild man: four-footed, hairy, mute
American: copper-colored, choleric, erect. Paints self. Regulated by custom.
European: fair, sanguine, brawny. Covered with close vestments. Governed by laws.
Asiatic: sooty, melancholy, rigid. Covered with loose garments. Governed by opinions.
African: black, phlegmatic, relaxed. Anoints himself with grease. Governed by caprice.

Readers may note the influence of Aristotle in Linneaus's scheme of races.

Aristotle believed health was maintained by a balance of the four humors (liquids) in the body and that individuals tended to be born with one humor predominating, influencing their natural temperament and personality. Linneaus's classification of races as choleric, sanguine, melancholy, or phlegmatic was a direct connection to Aristotle. Furthermore, Linneaus saw these differences resulting in predictable behavior patterns: "governed by caprice" is how he classified Africans. It was only a small step from "governed by caprice" to "slaves by nature." The idea of humanity being broken into races, as different as different species, was picked up throughout European cultures. For example, David Hume, the famous Scottish philosopher and a contemporary of Linneaus, wrote: "I am apt to suspect the negroes and in general all the other species of men (for there are four or five different kinds) to be naturally inferior to the whites. There never was a civilized nation of any other complexion than white" (quoted in Gould, 40–41).

SLAVERY AND RACE IN
THE ENGLISH-SPEAKING WORLD

As an economy supported by African slaves developed in the English-speaking world, the philosophy of race, especially of white supremacy, took hold, but the concept was eventually taken further than the Spanish had taken it. Many of the richest, most powerful people in England in the 1600s and 1700s were slavetraders, including many members of the House of Lords and the mayors of Liverpool and Bristol (Williams, 46–48). In 1774 the evangelist John Wesley cited statistics that about one hundred thousand slaves were being brought from Africa every year, with about thirty thousand dying en route (Wesley 1774, 21). Even though some of these slavetraders were men prominent in works of charity, Christian instruction of African slaves was discouraged and missionaries were actively persecuted (Coupland, 28–29). Unlike slaves under Spanish or Portuguese law, slaves under English law had no legal rights, marriages among slaves were not recognized, and slaves were ineligible as legal witnesses, except against another slave (Coupland, 29; Tannenbaum, 4–5), although there is also a question of how much the Spanish and Portuguese codes were obeyed by slaveowners (Davis, 69–83; Charles Darwin was one famous eyewitness of the cruelties of Brazilian slavery [Darwin, 20, 24–25, 496–98]). There was no question that in the English-speaking world, as a chief justice of St. Vincent noted, "White men are in a manner put beyond the reach of the law" (Coupland, 29). This can be illustrated by John Wesley's account of a Jamaican slave woman, about eighteen years old, who was punished by being stripped in a public square, hung by her hands with weights tied to her feet, and killed by whipping (Wesley 1774, 72).

English slavers often explicitly referred to blacks as nonhuman. For example, Edward Long, a Jamaican official, argued that African slaves should be classified with orangutans, "as a different species of the same genus" (Coupland, 28). In 1849 Thomas Carlyle, an influential English writer, produced an anti-abolition essay, "The Nigger Question," in which he concluded that blacks were "indolent, two-legged cattle" with "an indisputable and perpetual right to be compelled to do competent work for his living" (quoted in Williams, 195–96). Viewing people as domestic animals had practical moral and legal consequences. In 1781, the captain of a British slave ship, the Zong, decided he had a crisis—whether from disease or a shortage of resources is unclear—and he threw 132 slaves overboard to drown. The owners then applied for cargo insurance to pay for the lost slaves, and the case ultimately came before the highest courts in England. The British chief justice, Lord Mansfield, concurred with the owners on legal grounds: "no doubt, though it shocks one very much, that the case of slaves was the same as if horses had been thrown overboard" (Coupland, 60). The English were not alone: Arab slave traders operating in the Indian Ocean from the Middle Ages through the late 1800s had no reservations about throwing live African slaves overboard (Coupland, 212).

RACE AND CLASS: NOT ALL SLAVES WERE BLACK

Eric Williams, who later became prime minister of Trinidad and Tobago, wrote a detailed study, *Capitalism and Slavery,* on the rise and decline of slavery in the European colonies, especially in the British Empire. His central thesis is that slavery was economic rather than racial. In each of the countries involved, the machinery of exploitation was not initially set up with Africans. Later, after African slaves became the labor fueling the economy, the myth of superior and inferior races developed or was imported and eventually took on a life of its own. As we saw in our discussion of the Spanish *Conquista,* Native Americans were first exploited by the Spanish, and only as their populations plummeted due to introduced diseases were large numbers of African slaves brought in.

In England in the 1600s, capital punishment could be administered for pickpocketing, shoplifting, or poaching rabbits (Williams, 10). Consistent with mercantilism, the prevailing economic philosophy, an alternative was to put the poor and the convicted to work for the economic good of the nation. To this end, convicts were often sold as bondservants, especially from debtors' prison. According to Williams, the techniques of shipping human cargo to be used for labor were first developed for English bondservants, who might be locked below deck for an entire voyage across the Atlantic, each person confined to a space two feet by six feet (less than a meter by two meters). Just as kidnapping for slavery was common in Africa in the 1800s, kidnapping of the poor for export as bondservants was common in England in the 1600s. In 1670, Parliament even rejected a bill against the stealing of children for sale into this trade (Williams, 10–15). Later, as the Industrial Revolution began to develop in England, the value of the poor as a working class rose, and for American plantation owners it became cheaper to buy an African slave for life rather than an English bondservant for seven to ten years.

EVANGELICAL CHRISTIANS AGAINST THE SLAVE TRADE

The ending of the slave trade and the emancipation of slaves in the British Empire was heavily influenced by Christians, although economic and political forces also were at work. First public opinion and then policy were turned against the African slave trade by a coalition predominantly consisting of evangelical Christians, most often associated with one of their leaders in Parliament, William Wilberforce, a friend of John Wesley's (e.g., Dawson, 207–9). Wesley himself was strongly opposed to slavery. In his *Thoughts Upon Slavery* (1774) he documented horrors of the English slave trade and as a Christian attacked it. Williams criticized books such as Reginald Coupland's *The British Anti-Slavery Movement,* which attributed the success of abolition primarily to Wilberforce and other evangelical activists, as being simplistic and perhaps sentimental (Williams, 178, 211). Nonetheless, even a critic like Williams was convinced that the abolitionists were the "spearhead of the onslaught which destroyed the West Indian system and freed the Negro" (Williams, 178). There were a series of men whom Williams called "a brilliant band," less known to American Christians by name than was Wilberforce: Thomas Clarkson, James Stephen Sr., James Stephen Jr., James Ramsay, Granville Sharp, and others. All were friends of John Wesley, and all were dedicated to prayer.

Paul Goodman, in his study of American abolitionists, *Of One Blood*, has concluded that personal acquaintance with blacks often converted whites to the abolition cause. This was also true for some of the British abolitionists. Let us briefly consider one example of how personal acquaintance led to action on behalf of an individual, which led to questioning of the policy of the empire.

In 1765 Granville Sharp met a slave from Barbados named Jonathan Strong. His owner, a lawyer named David Lisle, had flogged Strong so severely he could barely walk, and Lisle had then pistol-whipped Strong's head so badly he was almost blind. Lisle had left Strong homeless, probably to die, in the streets of London. Sharp and his brother got him medical care, and when he recovered, found him a job. Two years later, Lisle encountered Strong, and because he was of value again, sold his title to a Jamaican planter, who kidnapped him. Sharp fought a lengthy legal battle that ultimately led to Jonathan Strong's permanent liberty and a fine levied on Lisle. However, Sharp was by then committed to the larger battle to abolish slavery (Coupland, 48–56).

In 1807 the slave trade was outlawed throughout the British Empire, in part because the sugar trade had been declining since the American Revolution and Caribbean plantation owners may have been more willing to relent on this point (Williams, 123). However, although sugar was not as profitable as it had been a century earlier, the slave trade was still profitable to the British economy, especially with the growing slave business in the United States (Fage, ix, the introduction to Coupland). Profits as high as 100% per voyage were possible, and profits less than 15% were rare (Williams, 36). Hence, the abolitionists had to fight and defeat a powerful economic lobby (Coupland, 37–38).

After the slave trade—that is, the sale of new slaves—was abolished, the issue became whether liberty of all existing slaves, or emancipation, was a realistic goal. The British abolitionists finally agreed on this by 1823, and by 1833 emancipation was proclaimed throughout most of the British Empire, with the exception of India (Williams, 182–85).

Whatever their shortcomings in getting to this point, by the 1830s the British navy was fighting the slave trade. Christian zeal continued to inspire a number of British foes of slavery, including Charles Gordon, who fought the Arab slave trade in the Sudan. The Muslim leader who killed him in 1885 immediately restored the trade in African slaves sold to Arabia and the Middle East (Coupland, 230–38). It is a cruel irony that Islam has gained in popularity among African Americans when the Arab slave traders were in sub-Saharan Africa long before the European powers were and continued capturing and selling black slaves long after the Europeans had repudiated slavery. In 1962 Saudi Arabia was one of the last countries to outlaw slavery, which by the twentieth century was almost exclusively Africans kidnapped from East Africa (Lewis, 79). In 1996 two reporters for the Baltimore Sun, one European American and the other African American, traveled into Sudan to investigate continued claims of thousands of black Sudanese being kidnapped and sold north as slaves; they succeeded, with relatively little difficulty, in purchasing the freedom of two black African slaves and saw first-hand evidence documenting a sizable slave business (Lewthwaite and Kane). In this case, the Muslim government in the north of Sudan is waging war on the Christians and practitioners of traditional religions in the south, and it makes extensive use of militias who are unpaid but allowed to keep the profits from any slaves they capture (Lewthwaite and Kane).

One of the main motivations of David Livingstone's journeys into East Africa was Christian evangelism and the ending of the slave trade (e.g., Coupland, 208). A former graduate student from Zimbabwe described for me the respect still accorded Livingstone. When the white supremacist party was defeated in the 1970s, primarily by two Marxist guerrilla organizations, and Rhodesia became Zimbabwe, monuments and street names of white conquerors throughout the country were destroyed. But not Livingston's monument: even the Marxists respected him as a man who lived simply and for justice and against the slave trade.

THE DEVELOPMENT OF SLAVERY BY RACE IN THE UNITED STATES

In the British colonies, before there were many African slaves, there were indentured servants, modeled in theory on Deuteronomy 15:12–18, in which slaves or bondservants were to be freed after seven years (Bennett, 36–38; Fredrickson 1981, 59–63). These people were mostly white, mostly poor, sent in bondage to the English colonies in North America sometimes for crimes, sometimes for debt, and sometimes kidnapped off the streets (Fredrickson 1981, 59–60; Williams, 9–11). Since the investment of the owner did not extend beyond seven years, the maximum usage of bondservants for hard labor was common, and many did not survive (Fredrickson 1981, 60). However, bondservants still had legal standing, whereas slaves, like prisoners of war, had no legal standing (Fredrickson 1981, 76). There is evidence that many of the earliest black slaves, imported to Virginia beginning in 1619, were freed after seven years in accordance with the concept of bondservanthood, especially if they were or had become Christians: that is, at that time Africans were perceived as being on an equal legal footing with English Christians (Fredrickson 1981, 76–78).

When the market for tobacco was increasing, the availability of English bondservants was decreasing for a variety of reasons, including the perceived need for labor in English factories (Fredrickson 1981, 60–63; Williams, 16–18). Nonetheless indentured servanthood persisted for a long time. As late as the 1690s, only about 25 percent of the bondlaborers in Virginia were black (Allen, 16). Similarly, in his travels through New Jersey in the early 1700s, John Woolman mentions bondservants purchased from places such as Scotland (e.g., Woolman, 24). It has been estimated that as many as half the English colonists to the future United States may have come as bondservants (Williams, 10–11). So, if someone comes from an English family line dating to the early colonial period, that person's ancestors may have been one more auctioned debtor or kidnapped peasant!

AMERICAN SLAVERY BECOMES BLACK SLAVERY

Although most slaveowners were white, some were not, but slavery in the future United States eventually came to rest on a racial philosophy. Slaveholders through the Civil War included some free blacks as well as several Native American peoples, some of whom had their own slave traditions that predated the European arrival, but the laws that developed prohibited the holding of white slaves by anyone (D'Souza, 74–79). After the mid-1600s, black skin color or African ancestry gradually came to be the mark of a population that could serve as slaves, even though there were free blacks.

The new philosophy of race produced spiritual byproducts. Various sources and court cases illustrate that a conflict developed between profitable slavery and the promotion of Christianity. The wealthy colonial elite of

Maryland and Virginia ultimately chose the path of greatest material profit (Fredrickson 1981, 78–80). Beginning in 1664, the Maryland and Virginia assemblies passed a series of laws that removed Christian faith as an exemption from lifetime bondage, potentially to all generations, for people of African descent (Fredrickson 1981, 78–80). The enormous profitability of tobacco and other plantation crops drove the development of a philosophy to justify black slavery after the slave market for Africans was an established fact. T. W. Allen suggests that this development may have been aided at least in part by fear on the part of the landed aristocracy that a union between black and white indentured servants might develop, such as occurred at least once in 1676 in an incident known as Bacon's Rebellion (Allen, 17).

Thus, by the 1700s, the English-speaking world had made a two-hundred-year journey from the biblical perspective of a single human race to the concept of several distinct races or subspecies, or perhaps even species, of humanity. Those with the palest skins had redefined themselves as both distinct and superior. This enabled people with a stake in Europe's ever-growing addiction to tobacco and sugar produced by human bondage to justify slavery. Although many Christians bought into the system, philosophically if not financially, not all did; and some spoke and acted for the God of justice who does not sleep but is patient, desiring repentance.

CHAPTER 4

—■—

Slavery and Abolition
in the United States

THE BIBLE DOES NOT SUPPORT ANY SYSTEM OF SLAVERY BASED ON differences in skin color or any other physical differences. Nonetheless, the ambiguous passage referring to Noah's curse on his son Ham (Genesis 9:20–27) was used as a meager justification and continues to live on in a few Christian circles, mostly as an oral tradition. By the early 1700s, Noah's curse was the justification being used in Virginia by English Christian slaveowners (Woolman, 55), just as we have seen that it was earlier used by Arab Muslim slaveowners from the Middle Ages. By the years before the Civil War, the concept had become a fully accepted part of the worldview of many whites. Among them was John C. Calhoun (1782–1850), a United States senator and vice president, who presented slavery of blacks as a "positive good" because there were "two races of different origin, and distinguished by color, and other physical differences, as well as intellectual" (Fredrickson 1981, 154).

What the Bible lacked, sometimes others filled in. Joseph Smith's *Book of Mormon*, claiming to be divine revelation, specified a dark skin as the mark of God's curse on some of the peoples named in its epic (I Nephi 12:33; II Nephi 5: 21–24). Brigham Young's words chillingly prefigure current kingdom identity theology: "Shall I tell you the law of God in regard to the African race? If the white man who belongs to the chosen seed mixes his blood with the seed of Cain, the penalty, under the law of God, is death on the spot" (Young, 10:110). But this theology was not restricted to Mormons. I. A. Beals gives an example of a supposedly evangelical theologian writing in the South in the 1920s, who believed that people of "mixed race" ancestry could never inherit everlasting life (Beals, 26–27).

29

LEGAL STATUS AS PART-HUMAN

The combination of the concept of an inferior black race destined for slavery and an orientation of the early United States government around the protection of property rights led to the provision in the Constitution that slaveowners would be granted three votes for every five slaves (Beals, 40–41). This was the basis for the 1857 Dred Scott decision by the U.S. Supreme Court that a black man was three-fifths human. In the words of Chief Justice Roger B. Taney, "Under the U.S. Constitution a black man had no rights which the white man was bound to respect . . . the negro might justly and lawfully be reduced to slavery for his benefit. He was bought and sold, and treated as an ordinary article of merchandise and traffic" (Beals, 71). With this underlying perspective, free blacks were not safe either: there were numerous cases of kidnapping of free men and women from Northern cities such as Philadelphia or New York for sale into slavery (e.g., Still, 361). For example, one such gang, based out of a tavern near present-day Reliance, Delaware, was run by a woman named Patty Cannon who was known to enjoy using torture on her captives, some of whom had been kidnapped from as far away as Philadelphia (Blockson, 147–48).

LIFE AS A SLAVE UNDER THE STARS AND STRIPES

What was life like as a slave in the United States? Many first-person accounts are available, and even more numerous second-person accounts, such as those recorded by Wiilliam Still (1871). John Wesley, who lived in Georgia for a time prior to the American Revolution, described atrocities that he witnessed firsthand or heard directly from others who were present. For example, a woman in North Carolina who attempted to run away was punished by being dragged behind a horse until she was dead (Wesley 1774, 71). A slave who resisted being sold in Charleston, South Carolina, was whipped until dead (Wesley 1774, 73). One owner cut off the ears of resistant slaves, boiled them, and would force the slaves to eat them (Wesley 1774, 46). A Virginia slaveowner roasted a runaway slave alive (Wesley 1774, 33).Two particularly well-written autobiographies by former slaves are *My Bondage and My Freedom*, by Frederick Douglass (1855) and *Incidents in the Life of a Slave Girl, Written by Herself*, by Harriet A. Jacobs (1861). Historical research has corroborated the accuracy of the accounts, as for example the extensive notes in the 1987 Harvard University

Press edition of Jacobs's book, in which many people referred to by aliases have been now identified by independent research.

Harriet Jacobs: Life for a Woman as a Slave

From her teen years on, Harriet Jacobs belonged to a medical doctor, James Norcom ("Dr. Flint"), who lived in Edenton, North Carolina. Edenton is in the coastal region of North Carolina, located only a few miles from Kitty Hawk, Duck, and other towns on the Outer Banks. Her family tree included whites and blacks; some of her relatives appeared white (e.g., Jacobs, 6). Her ancestors had tried for generations to purchase their freedom but were cheated several times at the last minute. She powerfully describes the moral degradation of the culture, although her parents and grandmother did all they could to rear her in Christian teaching. Dr. Norcum was an active member of the Episcopal church, yet he fathered at least eleven children by his slave women (35). His wife vented her frustration on the slaves rather than her husband, cursing one with a white-skinned child as she lay dying in childbirth (13). She would also spit in the kettles and pans with food left in them, so that no slaves would eat the food (12). A slave whose wife probably had a child by Dr. Norcum was hung from a beam and whipped for hours, apparently because of his anger at the doctor for the abuse of his wife. If Dr. Norcum was unhappy with a dish, he would cram the food down the throat of his cook until she choked (12).

From the time Jacobs was fifteen and Dr. Norcum was fifty-five, he began to try to force her to have sex with him, often requiring her to remain in his presence while he spoke to her at length in sexually explicit ways (e.g., 27–28; 32). Mrs. Norcum eventually pressured Jacobs into telling her about her husband's behavior (33). The Norcums' marriage continued to deteriorate, but so did conditions for Jacobs, although Dr. Norcum for years offered to maintain her as a mistress in a comfortable home if she would submit sexually to him.

Neighboring plantations are also described by Jacobs, such as several owned by members of a family named Coffield ("Litch"). The incidents she describes have been independently supported by other historical data (nn. 1, 3 and 4, 267–68). For example, on a Coffield plantation, slaves were sometimes hung by a rope while burning fat was dripped on them (46). Another Coffield brother would turn bloodhounds loose on runaways and allow them to kill the person (47). The destroyed families, black and white, are also described by Jacobs. White plantation wives generally chose to ignore their husbands' and sons' many affairs with slaves, or sometimes they would acknowledge the children openly but considered them a financial asset to be marketed, like piglets; only rarely was a family connection acknowledged (e.g., 36). Jacobs also knew a slaveowner whose daughter sought vengeance on her father by ordering a black slave to impregnate her, so that his first grandchild would be black (52).

To escape the advances of Dr. Norcum, Jacobs sought pregnancy with another man; she had two children by Samuel Tredwell Sawyer ("Mr. Sands"), who was later elected to Congress in 1837 (nn. X-1, XXIV-1, 268, 279). Much of her story from this time involves the manipulation of her children's possible freedom as a token in a game of will between herself and Dr. Norcum, until they were ultimately able to escape to the North, where she told her story to the world. Writing for a mostly white audience, her observations on the whole system deserve repeating as we consider the roots of evils with us yet in the United States:

> I can testify from my own experience and observation, that slavery is a curse to the whites as well as to the blacks. It makes the white fathers cruel and sensual; the sons violent and licentious; it contaminates the daughters and makes the wives wretched. And as for the colored race, it needs an abler pen than mine to describe the extremity of their sufferings, the depth of their degradation. Yet few slaveholders seem to be aware of the widespread moral ruin occasioned by this wicked system. Their talk is of blighted cotton crops—not of the blight on their children's souls. (Jacobs, 52)

Frederick Douglass: Life for a Man as a Slave

Frederick Douglass was born on the eastern shore of Maryland, the region today sometimes called the Delmarva Peninsula (i.e., Delaware-Maryland-Virginia). He grew up on a plantation owned by a Colonel Lloyd, near Easton, Maryland, a little south of where the present Chesapeake Bay bridge connects the peninsula with Washington, D. C.

Douglass's father was a white man (Douglass, 58), but Douglass never found out who his father was, and he was separated from his mother while still an infant (52). After that, his mother was able to visit him only occasionally, and usually illegally, by walking a long round trip at night from another plantation (53). He eloquently addresses fatherhood and slavery: "A person of some consequence here in the north, sometimes designated father, is literally abolished in slave law and slave practice" (35); "Slavery has no use for either fathers or families, and its laws do not recognize their existence" (51). Since, under the one-drop concept, the children of a black woman were also categorized as black and therefore slaves, he notes how this "gives to the pleasure of sin, the additional attraction of profit" (58). He describes the hatred of white wives for the children their husbands have conceived, often leading to the children being separated from their mother and sold far away (59).

American laws did not recognize slave marriages, and Christian slaves who desired to live a morally pure life, especially if they were beautiful women, faced a hard road (e.g., 86). One of Douglass's vivid childhood memories was of a beautiful woman named Esther who was in love with another slave, known to be a good man. She wished to marry him, but the master had other intentions for her. As a little boy, Douglass slept on the floor of a closet in the kitchen, and there he woke up early one morning to see Esther stripped to the waist, her hands tied to a rope hung from a beam in the kitchen, being whipped without mercy for the crime of sexual resistance (87). Because she still did not relent, other whippings followed (88). Douglass describes how a supposedly Christian master would lock a slave woman and man together, night after night, until the woman would be pregnant, as a "breeder" (218).

Douglass's faith in Christ for his salvation came at the same time he was discovering that abolitionists existed (162–66). He describes how, as a thirteen-year-old, he "felt the need of God, as a father and protector" (166). Both white and black Christians were involved in his conversion (166–69), and he describes how his life changed:

> I finally found the change of heart which comes by "casting all one's care" upon God, and by having faith in Jesus Christ, as the Redeemer, Friend, and Savior of all who diligently seek Him.
>
> After this I saw the world in a new light. I seemed to live in a new world, surrounded by new objects, and to be animated by new hopes and desires. I loved all mankind—slaveholders not excepted; though I abhorred slavery more than ever. . . . The desire for knowledge increased, and especially did I want a thorough acquaintance with the contents of the Bible. (Douglass, 166–67)

After his mother's death Douglass discovered that his mother had secretly learned to read—the only black in the area who could (57–58). This inspired him, and even more so after he had faith in Christ. He describes, for example, how while on errands in Baltimore, he found in the gutter some ripped, loose pages of the Bible—which as a slave he was not supposed to have access to—and he carefully washed and dried and saved these to read (167). He also met with an old black Christian who could read poorly but who seems to have been a remarkable man of continuous praise and prayer for his city (167–68). As Douglass grew in his skill in reading and his knowledge of the Bible, he wanted to teach others. He and a free black man named Mitchell and a white man named Wilson tried to start a literacy and Bible class for black children on Sundays in St. Michael's, Maryland, near Easton, but had it broken up by a white mob (199–200).

After many hard experiences, including a year in which he was sent to live with a man known as a "negro-breaker," Douglass succeeded in escaping to the North, where he became a major force in the abolition movement. While speaking at churches in England and Scotland, he wrote a stunning letter to his last master (421–28), in part concerning the treatment of his sisters, "for which you must give account at the bar of our common Father and Creator." The need for education for blacks continued to be a major emphasis in his speeches (e.g., 432). In spite of many obstacles, by the 1830s and 1840s at least some white Christians in several places, especially Ohio, began to develop significantly integrated schools or faculties for the first time in the history of the United States (Goodman, 253, 255).

GLIMPSES OF WHITE SLAVEOWNERS

Wendell Berry is a white American whose ancestors were Kentucky slaveowners. In the opening sections of *The Hidden Wound,* he relates a story about a tragic fate of one of their slaves that has been remembered by his family for generations. His family sold their slave and realized too late the new owner was a merciless man; he began beating his new possession before the slave left the Berry farm (6–9). Berry believes this story has never been forgotten because the family so regretted it. By owning slaves, even only a few, his ancestors were participating in a game with its own set of rules that they discovered they could not change even if they wished otherwise. The unresolved shame and guilt is a part of their family heritage.

Many of the artifacts of slavery in the United States can still be seen. One can visit old slave plantations, for example, and sometimes see the punishment cells and the balls and chains. Near Equality, Illinois, is one of the few slave plantations north of the Ohio River that is still standing and open to visitors. In the early 1800s, the owners were among the wealthiest people in the region, related to several presidents, and members of a local Protestant church. In a main hall, there is a mediocre painting of the slaveowner and his wife, a portrait that nonetheless succeeded in capturing their likenesses well enough to convey a strong sense of misery and hardness.

Besides owning slaves brought from the South, these slaveowners were part of an enterprise actively kidnapping slave refugees and free blacks who had gone further north in Illinois. The mansion was designed so that coaches bringing captives could pull up rapidly and unload the captives quickly through a special door. On the topmost floor there were tiny, windowless cells where resistant slaves or freedmen could be kept on hot summer days to break their wills. A visitor will also see the breeding rooms. This family chose certain black men to be the fathers of most of their slave offspring, whether the women were willing or not. On the wall is a photo, taken late in his life, of a man who had been used to sire more than one hundred children. Outside in the sun are the whipping post and various chaining systems.

This system exemplifies what Berry calls "short-order morality" (Berry, 106), as he explains:

> I believe . . . that the root of our racial problem in America is not racism. The root is in our inordinate desire to be superior—not to some inferior or subject people—but to our condition. We wish to rise above the sweat and bother of taking care of anything—of ourselves, of each other, or of our country. We did not enslave the African blacks because they were black, but because their labor promised to free us of the obligations of stewardship, and because they were unable to prevent us from enslaving them. . . .

It seems likely, then, that what we now call racism came about as a justification of slavery after the fact, not as its cause. We decided that blacks were inferior in order to persuade ourselves that it was all right to enslave them.

OPPOSITION TO SLAVERY IN THE UNITED STATES

An alternative worldview had begun developing by the mid-1600s, based on the Quaker emphasis of the New Testament principle of the equal standing of all peoples before God. One person who put this view into practice was William Penn, whose policy of liberty of conscience attracted Mennonites, Baptists, and Jews, as well as his fellow Quakers, to his colony. It was thus not illogical that Pennsylvania early became a focus for Christian opposition to slavery, especially the slavery based on the myth of an inferior race, although the first Quaker resolution against slavery occurred in Rhode Island rather than Pennsylvania, in 1652 (Beals, 5).

As in the Spanish-speaking world, some individuals were catalysts in abolition. One such an individual was John Woolman (1720–1772), a Quaker born in Mt. Holly, New Jersey—now near the suburban edges of greater Philadelphia—who traveled throughout the colonies as a preacher from the age of twenty-two. His personal record of his travels and thoughts, *The Journal of John Woolman,* was published after his death and continues to be considered a Christian classic. Readers familiar with eastern Pennsylvania, New Jersey, and Maryland will recognize many place names and be intrigued with the descriptions of life there 250 years ago. But the strongest impression his journal leaves is of intense spirituality, Woolman's desire that each person he met would be made right with Christ. Woolman seems to have used every opportunity to speak to people about their need of salvation and living by the Spirit of God. This was interwoven with a clear understanding that the presence of the Spirit of God must result in a changed life. He emphasized the spiritual hazards of accumulating wealth and the trappings of status as one element of this, but he especially focused on slavery as an evil. His journal often describes confrontations he had calling slaveowners to Christian repentance, to be evidenced by emancipation of their slaves. Like Las Casas, Woolman's social conscience could not be separated from devotion to Christ and evangelism.

"Abolitionist" and "Evangelical" Usually Went Together

The first official Quaker declaration in Pennsylvania against "buying and keeping of Negroes" was issued from Philadelphia in 1688 (Williams, 82). Progressively stronger steps were taken by the American Friends, until in 1776 the yearly meeting of Pennsylvania and New Jersey voted to bar

36

membership to slaveholders. By 1780 all Quakers in North America had freed any slaves they still owned (Williams, 83). Quakers such as John Greenleaf Whittier and Benjamin Lundy lectured and wrote aggressively against slavery, attracting national attention, sometimes violent attention. In 1838, for example, a pro-slavery mob in Philadelphia burned the head-quarters of the Anti-Slavery Movement where Whittier was editor (Williams, 181–85). In 1850 a white married couple in Baltimore suspected of aiding slaves to escape were tarred, feathered, and run out of town after a court acquitted them of the charge (Blockson, 83–84). Lucretia Mott was a Quaker minister active in the Underground Railroad in eastern Pennsylvania; when she and Douglass led an anti-slavery meeting in 1842 at the First Baptist Church of Norristown, Pennsylvania, a mob outside stoned the building (Blockson, 216). In 1857 a Methodist pastor in Cambridge, Maryland, was sentenced to ten years in prison merely for the crime of possessing maps of Canada, a popular destination for slave refugees, and a copy of *Uncle Tom's Cabin* (Blockson, 91–95).

It seems impossible to read accounts of the Underground Railroad, one of the most massive acts of civil disobedience in United States history, without reference to the faith and often biblical motivation of its participants, such as Douglass (e.g., Blockson, 99), or Harriet Tubman (Blockson, 103–6), or the Quaker women of Salem, New Jersey, who saw themselves fulfilling Jesus' command in Matthew 25 that what has not been done for "the least of these my brethren" has neglected Christ himself (Blockson, 219). Still, an African American from Philadelphia who was a leader in the Underground Railroad, wrote:

> There are many people who do not believe in the progress of religion. They are right in one respect. God's truth cannot be progressive because it is absolute, immutable and eternal. But the human race is struggling up to a higher comprehension of its own destiny and of the mysterious purposes of God so far as they are revealed to our finite intelligence. It is in this sense that religion is progressive. The Christianity of this age ought to be more intelligent than the Christianity of Calvin. (Still, 676)

The inner drive for abolition of slavery that eventually became a national movement was based in a desire to obey the lordship of Christ, just as it had been for Las Casas and Woolman. In 1832 William Lloyd Garrison, usually remembered for his political protests rather the foundation on which his advocacy was built, wrote: "there is power enough in the religion of Jesus Christ to melt down the most stubborn prejudices, to overthrow the highest walls of partition, to break the strongest caste. . . . 'In Christ Jesus, all are one: there is neither Jew nor Greek, there is neither bond nor free, there is neither male nor female'" (Frederickson 1968, 33).

John Wesley and the Methodists

As we have already seen, John Wesley and the Methodists in England were prominent in their opposition to slavery and racial ideas. In Wesley's journal, he recorded his reaction to American slavery: "I read of nothing like it in the heathen world, whether ancient or modern; and it infinitely exceeds, in every instance of barbarity, whatever Christian slaves suffer in Mahometan [Muslim] countries" (Wesley, February 12, 1772). For Wesley, the world was holistic: we find him, for example, moving directly from preaching on conscience to preaching on slavery (Wesley, March 3, 1788). On that particular occasion as he preached against slavery, there were a strange series of unexplainable, hostile phenomena in the meeting hall that Wesley believed was a demonic attack in response to his gospel assault on slavery. His response was spiritual:

> Satan fought, lest his kingdom should be delivered up. We set Friday apart as a day of fasting and praying that God would remember those poor outcasts of men; and (what seems impossible with men, considering the wealth and power of their oppressors) make a way for them to escape, and break their chains in sunder. (Wesley, March 3, 1788)

As Bartolomé de las Casas appealed to the civilizations of Native Americans to demonstrate their humanity, Wesley documented African cultures and political structure as clear evidence of their equality, and sometimes superiority, to European people (Wesley 1774, 7–15, 47). He stressed the common humanity of Africans and Europeans from a biblical perspective (Wesley 1774, 57) and that a just God must bring retribution, dealing with slavetraders and owners as they had dealt with their slaves (Wesley 1774, 51–53). Wesley not only prayed and preached but also advocated and supported political power. His last letter, for example, was written to his friend William Wilberforce, encouraging him: "Go on, in the name of God and the power of His might, till even American slavery (the vilest that ever saw the sun) shall vanish before it" (Wesley, February 24, 1791).

Some of the early Methodist evangelists had dramatic testimonies related to dealing with slavery. Freeborn Garrettson of Maryland, for example, inherited a prosperous plantation and slaves but declared them all free after his conversion. As he preached the gospel, nonviolence (in the midst of the American Revolution), and freedom for slaves, he was beaten, stoned, and sometimes jailed (Dawson, 64). By 1784 slaveowners and traders were to be excluded from membership in the American Methodists (Beals, 9; Dawson, 64–65), although pressure from Methodists living in states that forbade emancipation led to a compromise permitting slaveowners but not slavetraders to be Methodists (Dawson, 64–65). J. Dawson sees this event and similar compromises in most of the American denominations as a major blunting of the prophetic ministry of the church. Some of the most famous evangelical theologians of that day, such as Charles Hodge or James Henley Thornwell, were conspicuous by saying nothing on the subject of race or slavery, even as the nation slid toward the Civil War (personal communication with Allen Guelzo, Honors College, Eastern College).

Evangelical Christians Who Opposed Slavery Were at Odds with Society

As in the days of Las Casas, so too in the United States in the 1800s, there were Christian leaders of great vision, but many of the enfranchised, even though sometimes claiming Christianity, were opposed to the message such men brought. In Kentucky, for example, prayers were seldom said at the state legislature until the 1840s, because of the tendency of invited clergy to attack slavery; the separation of church and state was invoked in support of this (Berry, 15). James K. Polk, president from 1845 to 1849, opposed all religious teaching of his slaves (Dillon, 189).

Many well-known names among evangelical ministries occur in the lists of abolitionists. The theme of a life pleasing to God was linked with emancipation in Charles Grandison Finney's Revivals of Religion. Finney could not see revival separate from right relationships with God, and he insisted that slavery must end if revival were to come:

> Revivals are hindered when ministers and churches take wrong
> ground in regard to any question involving human rights. Take

the subject of SLAVERY, for instance. . . . Two millions . . . stretch their hands, all shackled and bleeding, and send forth to the Church of God, the agonizing cry for help. And shall the Church, in her efforts to reclaim and save the world, deafen her ears to this voice of agony and despair? . . . The fact is, that Slavery is, pre-eminently, the sin of the Church. . . . It is the Church that mainly supports this sin. Her united testimony upon the subject would settle the question. (Finney, 301, 303, 316)

As a young man, the future evangelist D. L. Moody tried to set free a fugitive slave being held in a Boston courthouse (Beals, 74). Phoebe Palmer, one of the first women to rise to national prominence in Christian ministry in the United States, focused on evangelism, personal holiness, and abolition in her meetings (Beals, 79). Gilbert Haven, a Methodist pastor and later a bishop, wrote a book in 1853 on the "absolute oneness of the race of man, in Adam, Noah and Christ." He advocated that Christians should welcome members of other races to their homes and accept interracial marriage as well (Beals, 83).

RACIAL DISCRIMINATION IN THE NORTH

Haven's radical stand based on Scripture alone was rare among white Christians, however. Many of the white churches in southeastern Pennsylvania, for example, did not aid escaping slaves, in spite of the prominent Underground Railroad movement there (Blockson, 205). Initially, many of the white abolitionists advocated returning freed slaves to Africa rather than developing a racially integrated country, although this policy was deeply opposed by most of the free black community (Goodman, 2). Although emancipation was declared everywhere north of Maryland during the American Revolution, there was a great deal of legal discrimination. In 1825, when Ohio became a state, it passed a law prohibiting blacks; both Virginia and Kentucky passed laws in 1806 giving free blacks one year to leave the state (Goodman, 5). White-only voting laws were passed in Connecticut, New York, Pennsylvania, and Rhode Island between 1814 and 1838 (Goodman, 7).

Douglass describes his surprise and hurt after reaching New Bedford, Connecticut, at being denied work in his trade (Douglass, 349), followed by finding the Lord's Supper segregated in the Methodist church there (pp. 350–53). He later describes his civil disobedience—eventually successful—

against Jim Crow railroad cars in New England (399–400). After her escape to the North, Jacobs had similar experiences throughout New York City and Albany or Rockaway; like Douglass, she stuck to her guns and was eventually treated equally in some settings (Jacobs, 175–77). Although Quakers freed their slaves, virtually none were welcomed into their churches or schools in the years following (Blockson, 205; Goodman, 7). In 1831 there was a proposal to develop a black school for training in the trades in New Haven, Connecticut, home of Yale University. With only four or five dissenting votes, the town, including many faculty members, voted to reject the school (Goodman, 47). A black preacher named Theodore S. Wright challenged the New York Antislavery Society in 1837 that what was becoming a mass movement against slavery was still not dedicated to treating blacks as equals in ordinary life (Goodman, 233–34).

Paul Goodman has written in *Of One Blood* on the development of belief in racial equality in America during this time. The thesis Goodman develops is that the change in perspective among many abolitionists was catalyzed by coming to personally know blacks. David Walker, a Methodist preacher who was the son of a white mother and a black slave father, wrote a book in the early 1800s, *Appeal to the Colored Citizens of the World,* in which he presented resistance as the test of human equality and attacked Christian hypocrisy in regard to racial discrimination. Walker believed that blacks were being given a ministry for the conversion of whites to see the colorblindness of the gospel (Goodman, 28–30). Samuel Cornish, an African American preacher, described his role influencing William Lloyd Garrison and other key abolitionists to accept complete equality of all peoples: "this doctrine is neither Tappan nor Garrison but is BIBLEISM, and we claim some instrumentality in teaching it to both these good men" (quoted in Goodman, 36).

RACE AND CLASS REVISITED: OPPRESSION BEGETS MORE OPPRESSION

Goodman also analyzed membership records for many abolitionist societies to understand the backgrounds of those who opposed slavery (Goodman, 137–72). He found that they were quite representative of many strata of society. Abolitionists generally perceived themselves as being aligned against an aristocratic mindset, North and South (Goodman, 137). Governor

George McDuffie of South Carolina defended slavery in a major speech associated with the presidential campaign of 1836: every society must have people to do menial work, a human "mudsill"; better that these be slaves than that they have enough freedom to organize labor strikes and have substantial voting power as was true among the poorest whites in the North (Goodman, 140–41; 154).

Goodman has documented a number of connections among the abolitionists and early stirrings for labor rights, such as the Workingmen's Party in New York City, whose leader, William Evans, appears to have been years ahead of much of the country in recognizing the implications of equality (Goodman, 163–67), or William Leggett, editor of the *New York Evening Post* and leading Jacksonian Democrat, who lost his job and his status as his abolitionist convictions deepened that the mindset of slaveowners did not lend itself to stopping with blacks (167–72). "We must put down slavery or it will put down us," he wrote (quoted in Goodman, 172). In at least a few instances, the camps of evangelical Christians, abolitionists, and labor union activists overlapped. The new Broadway Tabernacle, constructed only a year or two earlier for Finney's revival crusades, was used for a meeting of thousands of seamstresses organizing for better wages in New York's garment industry, a cause promoted by abolition papers (159–60). The abolition movement was the first time large numbers of women were mobilized in a cause in the United States, and for many it developed into the women's right movement (177–232).

Historians continue to debate all the reasons for the abolition of slavery, but it seems clear that in the United States and in England, the arguments of evangelical Christians primarily established the moral argument. In some Latin American countries, such as Nicaragua and Costa Rica, abolition of slavery came several decades before the American Civil War, in part a fruit of the appeal to conscience begun by Las Casas centuries earlier.

However, even as these victories were being won, new scientific models were developing that would be adopted to the defense of the concept of inferior races. In addition, the idea itself of separate races or human subspecies based on supposedly real differences was by this time accepted in much of the Western world.

CHAPTER 5

■

Development of Genetics as a Science

W

E WILL DEVOTE SOME ATTENTION TO IDEAS PRIOR TO THE DIS-
coveries by Gregor Mendel, as well as to Mendel's life and training, because they were important roots of his revolutionary
insights but also later contributed to misuse of his discoveries during the
twentieth century. Mendel is one of a small group of people who can truly
be said to have done something truly original, although the price he paid for
this was that no one seemed to have understood him until almost a generation after his death. Perhaps every culture has had some concept of *generation,* of how reproduction and the passing on of traits is controlled, but
until Mendel, no one seems to have understood correctly.

Prior to Mendel, speculations on the mechanisms of heredity tended to
follow one of two models. A classical Asian and Mediterranean concept
was that the female was the field whose womb nourished the offspring of
the male, the sower. The next generation was in the seed of the male; the
female was the passive recipient in which the seed was sown. This is
implied, for example, in the language of the ancient Hebrews (e.g., Genesis
29:31; 38:9; "seed" in the KJV), and in our biological term *sperm,* which
derives from the Greek *sperma,* for "seed."

Aristotle also believed this, but this prevailing concept was challenged five
centuries later by the Roman physician Galen, who had carefully studied
ovaries in dissections of animals and concluded they served the same function
as testes (Galen, 631–32). However, he did not know how heredity worked,
and he speculated that it was based on a blending of semen and a similar liq-
uid he reasoned must be produced by the ovaries. Galen had correctly perceived that both male and female contributed equally, but the resulting model
of heredity was that in each generation there was a complete blending of the
traits from the parents, rather like mixing liquids of two colors. The mixture

would appear somewhere between the two original liquids, and it would not be possible to reconstitute the originals once they had been blended. This was the predominant view in European science in the 1800s.

At the time of the German botanist Joseph Kolreuter (1733–1806), there was still a running debate whether plants were sexual organisms. For example, a Dr. Siegesbeck, a botanist at the University of St. Petersburg, wrote in 1737:

> What man will ever believe that God Almighty should have introduced such confusion, or rather such shameful whoredom, for the propagation of the reign of plants? Who will instruct young students in such a voluptuous system without scandal? (quoted in Olby, 19)

Kolreuter carried out experiments that demonstrated sexuality in plants (Olby, 25–35). Lab records have been discovered showing that several people after Kolreuter experimented with plant crosses and recorded observations similar to Mendel's, but no one seems to have realized the implications of what they saw (Olby, 37–85). Meanwhile, during the first half of the 1800s, Louis Pasteur (1822–1895) disproved spontaneous generation, the concept that life commonly arose from nonlife, and the cell theory, the understanding that all biological life is made of cells and all cells come from other cells, was being established by Lorenz Oken, Mathias Schleiden, Theodor Schwann, and Rudolf Virchow. These scientists established the basis for understanding that heredity must be based on a mechanism that used cells from male and female to carry and combine the hereditary information, whatever it might prove to be, into a new, blended cell.

GREGOR MENDEL AND THE KEYS TO HEREDITY

Gregor Mendel (1822–1884), born to a peasant family, became an Augustinian monk to enable himself to attend college, and later he taught biology and physics at a high school level. He was remembered by former students still alive in the early 1900s as a kind, conscientious, and talented science teacher (Olby, 114). Mendel's teachers at the University of Vienna included Christian Doppler (Doppler effect), a physicist who emphasized mathematical approaches to scientific problems (Olby, 113), and Franz Unger, a botanist interested in the cell theory, Kolreuter's work, and the studies in plant crosses—hybridization—done following Kolreuter's discoveries (Olby,

110–12). As a teacher and an Augustinian brother, Mendel had summers free, and he began to work on the problem of heredity, stitching all these ideas together. Using a mathematical approach that physicists, but not yet biologists, were used to, Mendel made crosses of pea varieties and followed individual traits in thousands of pea progeny over multiple generations. Although he published his work in 1865, no one understood it (apparently) until 1900, when it was rediscovered independently by three botanists in three separate countries.

Inheritance Controlled by Many Genes

Mendel discovered that inheritance is *particulate;* that is, each trait is controlled by some sort of discrete particles that are contributed by each parent and are transmitted generation after generation. This was different from the idea of inheritance being controlled by the male, or the idea that inheritance involved a blending in which the distinct characters of one generation would never be seen again. Mendel called these particles "elements," but they were later named "genes" (from the Latin root *gens,* found in words such as "generation"). Any trait controlled by a gene, such as the seed coat of a pea, could have more than one inherited form, such as a green or a yellow seed coat. We call these different forms of a gene alleles. Sometimes one of these *alleles* of a given gene was dominant in its expression when both were present. For example, when a pure-breeding yellow pea variety is crossed with a pure-breeding green variety, all the offspring in the first generation produce yellow seeds, but one quarter of the plants in the next generation will produce green seeds. That is, the trait for green seeds was not lost or blended with the yellow seed trait. Instead it kept its own identity, which enabled it to reappear in a subsequent generation under the right genetic conditions. In addition, Mendel demonstrated that the sex of the parent generally does not affect inheritance of a trait, which would not have been the case if inheritance was based on the male being like a sower and the female like a field.

INDEPENDENT ASSORTMENT

Another of Mendel's important discoveries was that the inheritance pattern of each trait is generally independent of that of other traits. This is called independent assortment. For Mendel's experiments, this was apparent, for example, in seed color being independent of smooth versus wrinkled pea types. In the second generation following the crossing of a green, wrinkled pea with a yellow, smooth pea, there will be seen the new combinations of yellow, wrinkled peas and green, smooth peas, in addition to the parental types of green, wrinkled peas and yellow, smooth peas.

By 1910 Mendel's proposed "particles" had been given the name *genes* and were shown to be carried on structures called *chromosomes,* inside the nucleus of the cell. We receive one set of chromosomes from our mother and one from our father, and thus we have two copies of each chromosome. Each chromosome is slightly different in size and structure, and they have been labeled. Humans have twenty-two pairs numbered 1 through 22 (e.g., chromosome 1, etc.), in addition to two sex chromosomes, X and Y, which determine whether a baby will be male or female (an XX baby will be a girl, and an XY baby will be a boy). In the production of human eggs or sperm, the chromosomes are divided in half, involving random separation of each chromosome pair. Thus, for example, if a single sperm has received the paternal origin chromosome 1, it could also receive the maternal origin chromosome 2, and so on, for all chromosome pairs. There can be any combination of chromosomes from a man's mother and father in any sperm cell. The same is true for a woman's egg cells.

An important application of independent assortment to the concept of races is that the presence or absence of any particular allele for one gene does not and cannot predict what the rest of the genetic material is like. There are some limited exceptions, such as the genes adjacent to each other on a single chromosome, which are more frequently inherited together, or linked. However, we as humans have 23 pairs of chromosomes, and only genes fairly close to each other on a single chromosome follow a linked inheritance—and even that breaks down with the passage of generations. This means that almost all of the approximately 80,000 human genes can be truly said to obey independent assortment. Imagine a deck of cards with 80,000 per suit instead of 13, and two suits, called mom and dad, for a total of 160,000 cards. Now shuffle that deck! Now do it again, many times, for each of the six billion or so people on the planet, as eggs and sperm are produced. After that, what are the odds that any one card will predict the next? As we saw in chapter 1, each conception is one combination of more than eight million times eight million possibilities for any two parents. Thus an allele for any one particular skin or hair color or bone structure can be combined endlessly with alleles for all the other components of our being that are controlled by DNA.

I once visited a small village in the rural Dominican Republic where a number of the people strikingly illustrated independent assortment of what people think of as European and African traits. Many of the people had longish faces and thin noses, often typical of European ancestry, and blue eyes and light blond hair were also fairly common among the people I met. However, that blond hair was often tightly coiled, like typical African hair ("nappy hair"), and the skin colors of the people tended to be brown. It was a handsome combination. Among the Native Australians, there are also people groups that have a high frequency of blond, straight hair, occurring with a dark brown to black skin.

GENETICS AFTER MENDEL

Since the rediscovery of Mendel's work in 1900, a great deal has been learned about heredity. We will refer later to the idea of genes controlling behaviors, so for those unfamiliar with the history of genetics, let us mention a few more of the pieces of the puzzle that have been fit together. By the 1940s, out of several component molecules present in chromosomes, DNA was demonstrated to be the molecule responsible for carrying genetic information. The physical structure of DNA was established in 1953, and the genetic code of the DNA was deciphered through the late 1950s and 1960s, permitting reading of the DNA into the language of the protein products of genes. DNA consists of long sequences of any one of four nitrogen-containing molecules, abbreviated as A, T, G, and C by geneticists who sometimes spend days poring over computer output consisting mostly of these four letters. As individual molecules, these are slightly alkaline or basic and thus are referred to as nitrogenous bases, or "bases." Each sequence is joined to a complementary strand, because each base will form an electrical attraction only with one other type of base: A and T are attracted to each other and bond, and so do G and C.

By the 1970s it was discovered how to easily move DNA among widely diverse organisms, and this has since been widely done for various research and commercial purposes, under the general label of genetic engineering. The last twenty years have seen an explosion of genetic knowledge, including the attempt being coordinated by the U.S. National Institute of Health to map the genes of humanity, the Human Genome Project. Differences in the DNA controlling any given trait are now understood to occur naturally to some degree and are due to any of several naturally occurring mutation mechanisms, as well as being provoked by damage to DNA from certain chemicals and certain types of radiation. Some groups of viruses and DNA regions known as *transposons* are also responsible for moving DNA sequences from one place to another, apparently occasionally among quite diverse organisms.

The ability to read DNA, to list out the message of a piece of DNA, molecule by molecule, has revealed many new insights. Among them is the discovery that for most genes there are not merely two or a few alleles within a species, but many, sometimes hundreds of small molecular variations on a theme. Many, perhaps most, variations in DNA do not affect quality of life. They do, however, permit more detailed studies than ever before of ancestral relationships, especially where there are unusual alleles that seem to have evolved within one ethnic group rather than being found in all human populations. Furthermore, it is now apparent that large portions of the chromosomes are not made of genes as we know them, but this non-gene DNA can also manifest small differences among different populations that can be used to propose the most likely movements and mixing of populations in history. We will make reference to both types of studies later in this book.

The first human trait that followed Mendel's rules was discerned in 1903, three years after his rediscovery. In 1909 work in wheat breeding showed how traits that follow the normal distribution, often called the bell-shaped curve, within a population can be explained by a species carrying multiple genes for a single trait, each of equal effect; this has been extended to explain how such quantitative traits as human height or skin color, traits that lack distinct categories like green seed coats versus yellow seed coats, produce a normal distribution curve on a population basis. In the normal curve, the majority of the population is found around the average or mean, with decreasing percentages found for extremes in either direction. Because the normal curve is fairly common in nature for physical measurements of populations of living things, statistics that assume a normal curve are also commonly used. However, the more the data are based on indirect estimates rather than on direct measurements, the less reliable that assumption becomes.

In summary, enormous progress has been made in understanding the physical mechanisms of heredity. Note, however, that essentially all of this understanding has come in the twentieth century, and the greatest part only in the last half of the century. It is now possible to compare ourselves not merely by a few outward characteristics such as skin or eye color but also at the unseen level of differences in DNA.

CHAPTER 6

■

Comparison Studies at the Level of DNA

I N RECENT DECADES TECHNOLOGY HAS BEEN DEVELOPED THAT permits comparison of genes at the level of individual molecule components of the DNA. One use of this powerful tool is to estimate how long different subgroups of a species have been separated.

When the DNA sequence changes, what we call a mutation, the bases on both long strands must have changed, and the expression used to describe this is a "base pair change." Large portions of the DNA in our chromosomes are not part of functional genes and seem capable of undergoing some small changes from mutations without noticeable effects. Possible pedigrees for groupings within a species can thus be developed by working backward, and some idea of the time involved can be estimated by comparing DNA variability within each of several different species, some of which may also have fossil data to assist in assigning dates.

If races were the result of humans developing as several distinct species or subspecies, one would expect different sets of DNA mutations within each race, just as species such as chimpanzees and gorillas differ, even though they may share many DNA similarities because they are primates. If the human race is one species, there could be some geographical mutation in which particular mutation forms were most common, but many alleles would occur in most populations, and there would be no clear and consistent boundaries among human groups based on sets of DNA differences.

Such work has been done based on sampling human DNA from many different ethnic groups across the planet. Besides comparisons of DNA in typical chromosomes in the nucleus, usually comparing a single gene or chromosome region, comparisons have also been made of Y chromosomes, carried only by men, and the DNA in mitochondria. Mitochondria are structures within each of our cells that are responsible for respiration. They are the furnace of the cell. Besides occurring inside their own tiny membrane outside the cell nucleus, they have their own chromosome and are almost exclusively inherited maternally, that is, inherited only from one's mother. The advantage of studying changes in mitochondrial DNA and Y chromosome DNA is that change in either must be due to new mutations, not recombination with a matching chromosome (see the section about genes in chapter 5). As we noted, for the rest of our chromosomes, there are two copies, one paternal in origin and one maternal. During the formation of sperm or eggs, each matched pair is capable of exchanging portions of DNA to produce novel chromosomes that are hybrids of the DNA from both parents, an intriguing process known as genetic recombination.

DNA COMPARISONS AMONG HUMAN POPULATIONS

There has been an enormous amount of work in this field, and we can only sample representative results. C. Stringer and R. McKie's *African Exodus* provides a thorough review of current understanding, as does the article by S. A. Tishkoff et al. in a briefer format. Probably the most thorough analysis of data on a global basis remains the work by L. L. Cavalli-Sforza, P. Menozzi, and A. Piazza, *The History and Geography of Human Genes*. For readers with a background in genetics, a 1997 article by J. L. Mountain and L. L. Cavalli-Sforza has a good discussion of the pros and cons of different research approaches in this field.

Based on various techniques to compare DNA samples, results have consistently shown that, for example, there are more DNA differences among related subspecies of chimpanzee, or even between any two neighboring gorillas in the African rainforest, than there are between any two humans, even from the most widely separated ethnic groups (e.g., Stringer and McKie, 116–17; 121–24; 131–35). K. K. Kidd and S. A. Tishkoff at Yale University and their many research collaborators around the world have been major contributors to this work. For example, Kidd et al. have shown that the whole human race outside Africa possesses only two variants of one region on one chromosome (chromosome 12), whereas in Africa, there are several possibilities: based on various estimates of mutation rate from these particular data, the dispersion of the human race could have occurred 90,000 years ago (Stringer and McKie, 132–36). A study of genetic diversity in a region of a different chromosome

(chromosome 11) showed that of 28 human populations sampled from every continent, each contained all the genetic variants found throughout the world (Kidd et al. 1998). In the African samples, however, each of the variants for chromosome 11 were also more common (Kidd et al. 1998).

Tishkoff et al. also compared variability in one particular region of chromosome 12, using blood samples from 1,600 people of many different ethnic origins. Their data strongly support a common human origin in Africa, with relatively limited genetic divergence since, within the time frame of 100,000 to 200,000 years ago. They found substantially greater numbers of alleles present in African peoples than in the rest of the world; no peoples sampled outside of Africa had alleles not also found in Africa, but each non-African people had less genetic variability than that found in any of the African peoples.

E. Zietkiewicz et al. (1997, 1998) compared genetic differences among 13 diverse human ethnic groups for a gene on the X chromosome. Most of the differences at this chromosome site were common to all samples. Unique DNA variations of the gene were mostly among the African samples. J. A. L. Armour et al. followed a DNA region with unusually frequent mutations among a diverse sample of 11 ethnic groups. (For geneticists, they followed a microsatellite region.) There was consistently less variation outside of Africa. Even distant ethnic groups like the Laplanders, or Saami, from northern Europe and Melanesians from the South Pacific shared common DNA characteristics for which differences existed among the African populations sampled. Based on the estimates of mutation rate of Armour et al., statistically the divergence of the human race could have been as recent as 15,000 years ago, although they suggest reasons why it was probably longer. Their data strongly support a common human origin in Africa, with relatively limited genetic divergence since, within a time frame of 100,000 to 200,000 years ago, based on estimated mutation rates.

M. Dean et al. compared variations at 257 different sites on the 23 human chromosomes, among four ethnic groups of Caucasian, African American, Chinese, and Native American (Cheyenne). Generally each of the four ethnic groups carried all variant forms of DNA for each site, although the percentages of each variant fluctuated among ethnic groups. The importance of all this work is that, had races or subspecies of humanity developed separately of each other in the very distant past, we would now expect completely different forms of DNA among ethnic groups at more of the sites, rather than generally the same sets of DNA variations for each. These results are most consistent with the development of the human race prior to the present separation of the ethnic groups.

Two recent studies comparing data for the Y chromosome are consistent with other studies. Comparison of human Y and chimpanzee Y showed 207 single base pair changes out of 15,680 base pairs in the Y chromosome (Whitfield et al.). Comparison of men from five widely divergent ethnic groups (Italian, Melanesian, Amazonian Indian, African !Kung, and Niger pygmy), however, revealed only three base pair changes among these diverse ethnic samples (Whitfield et al.). These data support the dispersion of the human race from a single, small population, possibly less than 100,000 years ago (Whitfield et al.). Using a different technique that permitted larger samples but not as much detail, M. F. Hammer estimated dispersion from a common population within the past 200,000 years, with the origin in Africa. A brief review of other recent work on Y chromosome diversity is given by A. Gibbons. Although these and other data show consistency in a geologically recent origin of the human race, beginning with a small, initial population, such as we encounter in the first chapters of Genesis, there is still some debate and ambiguity about the most correct interpretation of data in various cases. For readers interested in researching this area further, there is a good technical review of the data ambiguities and a critical review of the debate concerning a single human origin versus evolution of present humans from several origins by J. H. Relethford in the 1998 *Annual Review of Anthropology.* Relative to the overall theme of this book, however, the data do not seem ambiguous regarding the small amount of genetic variability in humans compared to most mammal species (Relethford).

Cavalli-Sforza et al., in their landmark study, *The History and Geography of Human Genes,* cataloged an immense amount of data, more than 70,000 frequencies of various genes in about 7,000 ethnic groups or subgroups, and correlated these with known data from linguistics, anatomy, and anthropology.

The basic approach of Cavalli-Sforza and his colleagues was to use advanced mathematical techniques to simultaneously compare allele frequencies for 45 genes among many different human populations. Most of the genetic traits they chose to follow are invisible to the eye, different forms of enzymes, for example, and in some cases there were a dozen or more alleles known by the time of their work (e.g., their table 1.3.1). The analyses of Cavalli-Sforza et al. show human populations as smudging into one another. When dozens of gene frequencies are followed simultaneously, boundaries among Africans, Asians, and Europeans disappear into series of gradations (e.g., their figs. 2.11.1–2.11.7). In what we could call the first cut of their global analysis, "the first principal component" that accounted for about 34% of the variance in their sample, Africa, the Middle East, and Europe form a single genetic set. That is, the rest of the world differed from the rather similar European and African gene frequencies (e.g., their fig. 2.11.1): Europeans and Africans share more DNA with each other in this analysis than they do with the rest of human populations. Native Americans, especially from South America, and Native Australians are the most genetically distinct humans, consistent with ocean barriers existing for millennia, but even in these peoples, the boundaries are not sharp with those of genes for the rest of the world. Their section on the "scientific failure of the concept of human races" (19–20) is a good abstract of the book:

> From a scientific point of view, the concept of race has failed to obtain any consensus; none is likely, given the gradual variation in existence. . . . The major stereotypes, all based on skin color, hair color and form, and facial traits, reflect superficial differences that are not confirmed by deeper analysis with more reliable genetic traits and whose origin dates from recent evolution most likely under the effects of climate and perhaps sexual selection. (19)

Cavalli-Sforza and his colleagues continue their work, incorporating improvements in technology as they become available. A recent example is a study based on DNA differences, many of these in regions outside of genes per se (Mountain and Cavalli-Sforza). Comparisons were made of 75 variations in DNA among 144 people representing 12 ethnic groups. Statistical analysis showed that genetic differences between any two individuals of a common ethnic background are often far greater than any among even very different origins. For example, the estimate of ethnic diversity between any two individuals in their sample of Italians was five times greater than that between any one of the Italians and a Japanese, an African, or a New Guinean. Some of the data in this study support the concept of Europeans as a mixture of DNA from Africa and Asia.

Briefly, then, data from comparison of DNA sequences support increasing diversity the closer one is to Africa, and in many cases the lack of diversity, compared with what is found in other mammals, shows that the human race is genetically of a common origin, a recent origin in terms of geological time, and there is a great deal of genetic similarity among all ethnic groups (Stringer and McKie, 136–46; Cavalli-Sforza et al.).

WHITE SKIN, AFRICAN ANCESTRY

In the fall of 1998, results of pedigree studies of the DNA of the descendants of Thomas Jefferson and his relatives and the descendants of Sally Hemings, a slave woman long alleged to have been Jefferson's lover after his wife's death, showed that at least one son, Eston Jefferson, was fathered by him (Foster et al.). Hemings herself was the half-sister of Jefferson's wife: that is, she was the daughter of a slave and Jefferson's father-in-law. These particular descendants of Sally Hemings have considered themselves white for generations and included a Union officer wounded at the battle of Vicksburg (Murray and Duffy). For other children of Sally Hemings and, probably, Thomas Jefferson, arrangements were made during Jefferson's life for several to "run away" and disappear into white society. Two daughters, Beverly and Harriet, disappeared so effectively that their subsequent history and that of any descendants is unknown (Edwards 1998). In the line descended from another son, Madison, some developed white family identities, changed their names, and disappeared from the genealogy, whereas others kept a black identity, including one descendent who was California's first black state legislator (Edwards 1998; Murray and Duffy). Yet another son of Sally Hemings, Thomas, stayed within the black community and became an African Methodist pastor (Edwards 1998).

Eugene Genovese has written one of the definitive historical studies on the life of the black slaves in the Old South, *Roll, Jordan, Roll,* and he devotes a chapter to what was referred to as "miscegenation" (Genovese, 413–31). The one-drop laws, such as 1/64 ancestry, defined a Negro in Louisiana, but Genovese suggests that in most Southern states it was 1/4 or 1/8 because of the danger of embarrassing leading white families if investigations were pushed much further (Genovese, 420). In South Carolina and among the early Afrikaners in South Africa, there was not a pedigree rule (Fredrickson 1981, 111–24). In South Carolina, a critical court decision stated: "The condition is not to be determined solely by visible mixture . . . but by reputation. . . . It may be . . . that a man of worth . . . should have the rank of white man" (quoted in Fredrickson 1981, 120). G. M. Fredrickson (1981) cites a number of studies documenting African and Asian ancestry in as much as 25% of the oldest Afrikaner families, with one researcher estimating Afrikaners are about 7% African and Asian or "nonwhite" (cited on 119).

We saw how it is possible to follow small differences in DNA sequences among different populations, to suggest likely ancestral origins. These same techniques have also revealed a general lack of boundaries among the world's peoples. Although they are not as accurate as DNA data, forensic data have also sometimes been used. For example, measurements of ancient Egyptian skulls revealed African, European, and many intermediate patterns (Ortíz de Montellano, 34). These and the data that are summarized below are consistent with the mixing of the world's blood during thousands of complex family histories, like the Jefferson and Hemings history, and perhaps yours and mine. Sometimes these have confirmed oral histories as well. Let us examine some representative studies.

MORE STUDIES ON THE MIXING OF THE WORLD'S PEOPLES

Studies of variations in DNA sequences among Brazilians have suggested that Brazilians considered white have between 10% and 33% African and/or Native American DNA, depending on the region of Brazil; among Brazilian blacks, as much as 50% or more of an individual's DNA may be of European origin (Franco, Weimer, and Salzano). Studies of DNA in two Brazilian and one Venezuelan populations of people considering themselves black indicated that they carried 18% to 28% white DNA and 3% to 32% Native American DNA (Bortolini et al.). DNA analysis of African Americans in Pittsburgh, Pennsylvania, suggested they carried about 25% European DNA (Chakraborty et al.).

An interesting example for students of the Bible is the Lemba. The Lemba are a Bantu-speaking, dark-skinned people, native to Southern Africa and Zimbabwe, whose oral tradition maintains they originated as traders and craftsmen far to the north but were cut off from their homeland by an invader. Their food laws are basically kosher, and details of their oral traditions fit with the events of the first exile following the Babylonian captivity of Jerusalem. Analysis of DNA sequences for selected regions, especially on the Y chromosome and the mitochondrial DNA, indicated that the majority of the Y chromosomes were Jewish in origin, whereas the mitochondria were all black African in origin. This confirmed their own oral history that the ancestors of the Lemba were men on trading expeditions, probably from Jewish trading bases in the Sabean Empire in the Arabian Peninsula, suddenly cut off from return to their homeland, who took local wives and settled down (Spurdle and Jenkins).

Studies of the mitochondrial DNA among populations in India were compared with studies of other Indo-European and Asian peoples. These data showed that the Asian Indians were clearly predominantly Caucasian or European in their specific DNA sequences, although with East Asian DNA mixed in (Barnabas, Apte, and Suresh) Given the historical importance of skin color in the United States, this study is a good example of how superficial it is as a genetic trait: the Asian Indians, although generally darker-skinned than Middle Eastern and European peoples, are clearly descendants of the same ancestors, as long suggested by language clues (e.g., Barnabas, Apte, and Suresh; Cavalli-Sforza). Even among northern Europeans, the Nazis' supposed purebred blond Aryan ideal, we find that a study of variation in one of the important genes in resistance to cancer, revealed evidence of Asian genetic influence among some of these peoples (Birgander et al.).

Based on combined analysis of data for various allele frequencies, it was estimated that Puerto Ricans are genetically a mixture of about 45% European, 37% African, and 18% Native American DNA; for Cubans and Mexican Americans, the contributions of these same peoples were 62%, 20%, and 18% for the Cubans and 61%, 8%, and 31% for the Mexican Americans (Hamsitis et al). Similar results for Mexican Americans were obtained in study by J. C. Long et al.

RACE A MEANINGLESS CATEGORY

Assume that races—radically different subspecies of human—had once been real, even though we know the data about genetic variation among human nationalities do not support such a theory. Even had races once existed, today hundreds of millions of people no longer fit in one category. Entire nations and ethnic identities are increasingly blends of the races: Mexicans, Brazilians, Venezuelans, Louisiana Cajuns, perhaps all the present peoples of the Caribbean and the Pacific islands. With each passing decade, the old categories are becoming less useful in describing people. In the United States, government census data indicate about 5% of blacks are currently marrying whites, resulting in tens of thousands of births per year of children with a black and a white parent; about 25% of Hispanics and about 33% of Asians also marry "outside their ethnic group" (D'Souza, 552). Our categories of race were always more falsehood than truth, but God's category stands: "God so loved the [one] world that he gave his one and only Son, that whoever believes in him shall not perish but have eternal life" (John 3:16).

One common estimate of human DNA content is that we carry about three billion base pairs (Human Genome Project), each base pair being potentially a single letter in a genetic message. How well do you yourself know who contributed to the three billion letters in your genetic message? Close to half of your DNA came from your mother and the rest from your father. It's not exactly half and half, because the mitochondrial DNA comes only through the mother, and the X chromosome is larger than the Y chromosome. For these reasons, there is slightly more maternal DNA than paternal DNA in each of us. Because girls receive two X chromosomes and boys one X and one smaller Y chromosome, the ratio of maternal/paternal DNA is slightly greater in girls than in boys.

But what about earlier generations? What do you know, for example, about the grandparents of your grandparents? There were as many as sixteen of them. Each of these sixteen people potentially contributed more than 100 million base pairs of your present DNA. Extend this consideration of your family tree back ten generations, which would generally be less than five hundred years, not very long in human history. To understand your ancestry, you would potentially have to account for 1,024 ancestors (almost certainly somewhat less because most of us are descended from people who lived in rural areas and shared a number of recent ancestors). Each of those people could still potentially account for about 3 million base pairs of your DNA. Because the sorting of chromosomes is random when sperm and eggs are made, some contributed more to your DNA and others less. But do you have any idea who any of them were, let alone from whom you inherited more and not less DNA?

Thus, it is becoming increasingly evident that all of us are mixtures of many unknown ancestors and that there have never been boundaries among peoples that prevent the birth of children of mixed ethnic backgrounds.

GENETIC AND ENVIRONMENTAL COMPONENTS OF INTELLIGENCE AND PERSONALITY

The best data, based on comparisons of test scores, especially among blood relatives, show that a genetic component, probably the result of a number of genes, does play a measurable role in the human persona. The limitations of all test score data, for any index of linguistic intelligence, spatial intelligence, interest inventories, emotions, or other qualities must always be kept in mind, but with that caveat, the results to date indicate that both heredity and environment are important. R. Plomin's work, although now a little dated (1990), gives a good review of the general field.

Some of the best work has been done by the group headed by Thomas Bouchard at the University of Minnesota. They have focused on comparing identical twins with fraternal twins; identical twins are genetically clones, their DNA sequences are completely alike. Situations in which identical twins were separated at birth or shortly afterward and not reunited until adulthood permits some comparison of environmental effects relative to genetic effects, on any trait of interest.

Bouchard's group has facilitated such reunions and now has a database of 64 such pairs of identical twins and 32 such pairs of same sex-fraternal twins (Bouchard et al.; Fox et al.). Besides completing contemporary adult versions of the IQ, twins spend more than 50 hours completing tests of many kinds, as well as being examined medically (Bouchard et al.). For identical twins reared apart, the correlation of IQ scores was almost 0.70; correlation of speed of spatial processing was 0.36; correlation of the Strong Campbell Interest Inventory, an index related to motivations toward different types of work, was 0.39; correlation of "religiosity scales" was about 0.50; etc. (Bouchard et al.). Correlation is a measurement of how two variables are related to each other. For example, one's height is strongly correlated with distance from fingertip to fingertip when one stands with arms outstretched. A correlation of 1.0 indicates complete identity; a correlation of 0.0, complete randomness. If the correlation value is squared, one gets an estimate of how much the correlation explains variability in two traits. Thus, the correlation of IQ scores above 0.70 indicates that about 49% (0.7^2) of the relation between separated identical twins could be attributed to their identical genes and not to their environment.

Bouchard has published a tabulated comparison of "personality determinants" (indices of openness, agreeableness) and their heritability correlations among twins (Bouchard): the values are generally in the range 0.40 to 0.50. Similar estimates of the heritability of "acquisition of motor skills" were about 0.66 (Fox et al.).

While I appreciate the elegance of the research from Bouchard's group, I must point out that their analyses, too, are partly based on running statistics of statistics. That is, when Bouchard presents a table cataloging the degree of inheritance of "openness" (e.g., Bouchard), he is measuring the heritability of an index score from various questions believed to estimate openness, not the actual genetic differences that influence mental attitudes in some way. An index is a number made by summarizing many values through some type of formula. A test score is a simple type of index: results for right answers on various types of questions are summarized into one number. When Mendel counted peas, "15" unambiguously meant 15 peas, and "0" meant no peas. In contrast, an index constructed to measure "openness" will always be indirect data made of many scores, in which equivalent score differences between two "open" people may exist for very different reasons than for an equivalent score difference between two "closed" people; in addition, a score of "0" would not mean the person has no personality!

The amount of variability *not* explained by a correlation is generally estimated by 1 minus the correlation squared. Thus, for example, about 51% of the variability in IQ scores for this sample of identical twins, reared apart, would *not* be attributed to genetic origins (that is, 1 minus 0.70 squared), and about 85% of the variability in the Strong Campbell Interest Inventory results would *not* be explained by common genetic origin. No two individuals are ever as similar genetically as identical twins; hence, correlations among measures for any traits would be expected to be far smaller among all other people, even of the same family.

Bouchard and his associates, however, generally tend to be reasonable in the presentation of their results. In the paper (i.e., Bouchard et al. 1990) that reviews their results over a period of years, they summarize their conclusions as "It is a plausible hypothesis that genetic differences affect psychological differences largely indirectly, by influencing the effective environment of the developing child. This evidence for the strong heritability of most psychological traits, sensibly construed, does not detract from the value or importance of parenting, education, and other propaedeutic [introductory instruction] interventions." Other papers from Bouchard and his colleagues and former graduate students (e.g., DiLalla et al.; Lykken et al.) have built an impressive case for uniquely individual gene combinations that result in positive traits (Lykken et al.) as well as cases of mental illness (DiLalla et al.). D. T. Lykken et al. have even coined a new term for this, "emergenesis," by which they mean that "unpredictable properties"—individually unique personalities, talents, and weaknesses—emerge from the countless interactions of the thousands of gene versions combined together for the first time in each new conception.

In summary, although a genetic component, or we could say a genetic influence, can be shown to exist for many human personality traits, it exists as a statistical estimate. For each such estimate, a large portion of the variability, often the largest portion, is not accounted for by genetic differences. In addition, although the genetic component behind the statistic must still ultimately be made up of individual genes—it would still follow Mendel's insights about particulate inheritance—there are so many genes involved in any trait as multidimensional as intelligence that a simplistic approach that assumes there are consistently smart and dumb family trees is nothing less than self-deceiving.

As C. Fyfe points out in his insightful essay, the only way that race can be usable as an instrument of social policy is if race can be correlated with behavior. That is, if one knows the race of an individual, that person's abilities and behavior would be predictable. The best data we now have show that even for those completely genetically identical, the effect of different environments on such traits is often as large or larger than the genetic component. The lives of different children from the same parents cannot be predicted genetically—how much less children from around the world!

At the level of DNA, we are one human race, not several. However, during the 1800s and much of the 1900s, as Europeans and their descendants dominated the planet, it was easy to believe in a distinct and superior race, identified by the simple trait of skin color. Wasn't the moral lesson of evolution that aggressive domination over the weak was the secret of the universe?

CHAPTER 7

■

Evolutionary Genetics as
an Argument for Racial Superiority

ALTHOUGH THE LIBRARY OF CHARLES DARWIN (1809–1882) included the book with Mendel's paper, Darwin apparently never understood Mendel's work. Darwin was a brilliant man with wide-ranging interests, but, like Christopher Columbus, his accomplishments have been somewhat mixed with myth. The shape of the earth was already known to literate Europeans of Columbus's time, and numerous academics were speculating on evolutionary divergence of organisms prior to Darwin: the achievement of both men was demonstrating what had already been discussed abstractly. In Darwin's case, the independent development of the same ideas by Alfred Russel Wallace (1823–1913) stimulated the publication of his most famous book, *The Origin of Species by Means of Natural Selection* (1859). Wallace, who had been doing biological collecting in Southeast Asia after traveling extensively in South America, had sent a copy of a manuscript outlining his ideas to Darwin to review. Wallace later graciously ceded academic precedence to Darwin, based on the fact that Darwin had worked on the topic for many more years following his own travels and biological studies in South America, the Pacific, and tropical Asia, although he had hesitated to publish for fear of the controversy it would bring. In present-day college texts, both men are commonly given credit together.

THE CONCEPT OF EVOLUTION
BY NATURAL SELECTION

The basic framework of Darwin and Wallace is fairly simple: more offspring are produced than the environment can support; there is natural variation within every population; the surviving offspring tend to be those that are more fit or adapted to the stresses of their particular environment; and over long periods of time, many accumulated small changes have resulted in the present biological diversity that we see. The whole scheme was eventually popularized by the British philosopher Herbert Spencer as "survival of the fittest."

What Darwin's worldview was has been hotly debated: it varied somewhat from book to book and letter to letter, and he wrote volumes on many subjects. His maternal grandfather, Josiah Wedgwood, founder of the pottery enterprise, was an active abolitionist (Coupland, 94), and we know that Darwin himself hated the enslavement of Africans as an atrocity (e.g., Darwin, 496–98). In his 1996 revision of *The Mismeasure of Man*, Stephen Jay Gould includes a new essay analyzing Darwin's views of other peoples, which Gould interprets as paternalistic but generally not racist, at least not as a consistent worldview (Gould 1996, 413–24). Whatever Darwin believed privately, however, the concept of evolution was soon popularly understood in terms of progress in a chain of being, an idea of hierarchy applied to biology to justify racism.

Following the rediscovery of Mendel and the refinement of disciplines such as population genetics, a new synthesis of evolutionary concepts developed. In addition to selection for adaptive advantages, there is recognition of the equal or greater importance of random genetic changes due to isolation of small populations, and perhaps also from occasional unexpected emergent properties of certain novel genetic combinations. The importance of catastrophes in wiping out many species otherwise fit is also recognized. Some of these catastrophes probably were planetary in scope, such as whatever it was that is believed to have hit the earth and defined the end of the dinosaurs. Sometimes this new evolutionary synthesis has been described, only partly tongue in cheek, as "survival of the survivors."

If we apply this current understanding to human history, most of the physical differences among the ethnic groups of the world thus reflect the fact that migrating peoples usually traveled in small bands that carried only a portion of all the diversity the human race possesses. Physical traits that predominate in any particular ethnic group probably reflect whatever mix of genes for appearance a small migrating clan possessed thousands of years ago, rather than being clues to the super race. There are a few instances in which human evolution for better survival in a harsh environment seems to have occurred within a particular ethnic group, but these mostly concern traits that do not involve outward appearance, such as the ability to handle low oxygen at high altitudes among the Sherpas in the Himalayas or the Quechua in the Andes.

However, one hundred years ago the prevailing assumptions about race made it an easy step to assume that superiority and inferiority might follow Mendel's rules, just as yellow and green seed coats in peas did. Just as evolutionary forces shaped the finches Darwin studied on the Galapagos Islands, by changing their gene frequencies, perhaps so had generations of selection through struggle and war selected the northern Europeans to rule the species. Or so the Europeans wished to believe.

"RACE" AS AN EXPRESSION OF EVOLUTIONARY GENETIC PROGRESS

During the centuries after the concept of race, and more particularly, the race superiority of the Europeans, was established in Western thought, a vacuum of authority to support the concept developed as the prestige of the classical philosophers declined. As we saw, during the Spanish Conquista the words of Aristotle served as the original scholarly justification. As modern science became solidly established and numerous errors were found in the natural science of the ancient Greeks, Aristotle gradually faded from use as a reliable scientific authority.

However, rather than acknowledge the full humanity of all men and women, what filled the gap left by the decline of Aristotle's prestige was a sequence of ideas and studies often backed by much of the scientific community but ultimately lacking scientific truth. As each defense by the scientific community of the concept of race fell apart, another was proposed, often became popularized, and later would collapse as irrefutable experimental data revealed errors. After the ideas of Darwin and Wallace had become incorporated into science, racial superiority tended to be robed in the language of evolutionary struggle, and after the rediscovery of Mendel's work, in the idea that the difference between superior and inferior might be as simple as a single gene.

HAECKEL'S APPLICATIONS OF EVOLUTION AS SCIENCE AND PHILOSOPHY

In the early 1860s, Ernst Haeckel, the German zoologist who coined the term ecology to replace the phrase "economy of nature," encountered The Origin of Species. In Darwin's ideas, Haeckel found the answer to Germany's future, through evolutionary struggle. He also coined the term "Mongoloid idiot," based on his belief that this genetic disorder, now called Trisomy 21, reflected a throwback to a more "primitive race"—the Asians—because of the superficially similar eyefolds. Haeckel's perceptions of Jews and Christians can be illustrated by his belief that Jews were biologically incapable of participating fully in German culture and that Jesus was the offspring of a Roman who seduced Mary (e.g., Shipman, 93–95).

Haeckel invented the term monism to describe his concept of the oneness of the universe. His application of evolution to the universe included the evolution of the human soul, which he speculated was a "state-soul" derived from countless little "cell-souls." From his interpretation of evolution Haeckel attacked the idea of the equality of humanity; he believed in the superior Aryan race, blond supermen who were destined by a Force within the universe to rule (e.g., Shipman, 93–95). Democracy was not consistent with good science, either, according to Haeckel: "The human will has no more freedom than that of the higher animals, from which it differs only in degree and not in kind . . . the greater the freedom, the stronger must be the order" (Haeckel, quoted in Burke, 265).

Although today he is sometimes only mentioned in passing for coining the word ecology, in 1906 Haeckel founded the Monist League, which brought together German intellectuals of many backgrounds to work toward policies based on the inevitability of racial struggle and the superiority of the German peoples (Burke, 266). Here, then, is the perspective on the relative value of human life by one of the most respected biologists of the late 1800s, both inside Germany and out, from his best-selling *Wonders of Life* (1904): "lower races (such as the Veddahs [of India] or Australian Negroes) are psychologically nearer to the mammals (apes and dogs) than to civilized Europeans; we must, therefore, assign a totally different value to their lives" (quoted in Shipman, 102).

The Monist League shortly joined with fourteen other "free thought" groups in Germany to form the Weimar Kartel, an anti-Christian organization, because the church was perceived as being the main social force protecting the evolutionary unfit. Haeckel was also one of the honorary chairs of a scientific society founded in 1900, the Society for Racial Hygiene, which had its own refereed journal, the *Journal of Racial and Social Biology*. The society eventually attracted thousands of members, including many intellectuals from German universities (Shipman, 132).

In *The Evolution of Racism*, Shipman concludes that the German scientific community created the Nazi Party, rather than the Nazi Party forcing itself on the scientific community (135). *The Handbook for Hitler Youth* began by spending large amounts of time teaching Darwin, Mendel, and Haeckel, to be applied later as the justification for Nazi policies (Shipman, 135).

Haeckel's application of Darwin's construct to support racial superiority fit ideas that were already in currency. William Shirer's *Rise and Fall of the Third Reich* remains an excellent review for Germany: Johann Fichte and Georg Hegel at the University of Berlin and their dream of the "German race" that would bring forth "heroes" to "carry out the will of the world spirit" (Shirer, 98); Nietzsche and his idea of the "superman," "a daring and ruler race is building itself up" (Shirer, 100); and especially Arthur de Gobineau. Gobineau was a French diplomat who worked briefly with Alexis de Tocqueville, author of *Democracy in America*. Gobineau later published a four-volume work in the 1850s, *Essay on the Inequality of the Human Races* (Shirer, 103). "History shows that all civilization flows from the white race, that no civilization can exist without the cooperation of this race," said Gobineau (quoted in Shirer, 103). For Gobineau and the Nazis, who adopted his philosophy as their own, racial superiority was determined by a lack of mixture with other races: the Germans theoretically were still mostly pure Aryan, the mythical ancestors of the white race, and thus strong to conquer, whereas the Latin peoples and other peoples of the ancient classical empires in the Middle East had once been white but were now weak and unfit to rule because they had become racially mixed.

In Adolf Hitler's words, "The highest purpose of a folkish state is concern for preservation of those original racial elements which bestow culture and create the beauty and dignity of a higher mankind"; "We all sense that in the distant future humanity must be faced by problems which only a highest race, become master people and supported by the means and possibilities of an entire globe, will be equipped to overcome" (quoted in Shirer, 89). Under the Nazis, all universities set up departments in "racial science" (Shirer, 250), and the majority of university professors, including the well-known philosopher Martin Heidegger (Shirer, 251), took an oath of loyalty to Hitler. There is evidence that Hitler sometimes directly plagiarized speeches from Haeckel's books (Shipman, 134).

Before the Jews and Gypsies began to be shipped off in cattle cars to be exterminated, the transformation of German medicine occurred. There was extensive propaganda by the Nazi Party that it was a kindness to eliminate the "unfit." By 1939, the laws had been changed to allow doctors and nurses to choose when the death of a handicapped or retarded child was justified. This was soon expanded to include adult psychiatric patients (based on the idea that mental illness is largely genetic). Data suggest that by 1941 more than seventy thousand such acts of kindness had occurred, all without official government orders to do so (Shipman, 138). Perhaps it was then only a small step to extend compassion to the Jews and Gypsies and others, who surely would have concurred, had they only shared the same scientific perspective.

Hollywood imagery has often pictured the Nazis as evil neurotics who stomped around in boots, clicking their heels, angrily spitting out their words. However, most of the leading lights of natural science and naturalism in the Western world were almost equally racist in their thinking, at least through the end of World War II. The sins of the German fascists differed in degree more than in kind from even the United States; the Nazis surpassed in quantity and official government sanction all other countries in deaths and oppression for a racial cause, but smaller numbers of deaths and atrocities were simultaneously occurring in the United States and elsewhere based on the same rationalizations. Let us examine some of the prominent scientists and others who influenced this type of thinking.

GALTON'S VIEWS OF EMINENCE AND RACE

Francis Galton was a British scientist and a cousin of Charles Darwin who discovered, among other things, that fingerprints are totally individual. In 1869, Galton published *Hereditary Genius,* in which he applied the developing concept of the normal curve, the bell-shaped curve, to a hypothesis about the inheritance of human traits such as eminence. He began with this foundation: "The general plan of my argument is to show that high reputation is a pretty accurate test of high ability" (Galton, 45–46). Based on studies of the pedigrees of people who had eminent reputations, mostly from within English and American society, Galton concluded that genius is highly heritable. In fact, he concluded that many of the eminent English were related (46); his work was summed up by later authors as finding that about half the great men of England had distinguished close relatives (Poponoe and Johnson, 16). This implied for Galton that nature was more important than nurture; the result could easily be extended to imply that this small group of men was the genesis of the future super race. The possibility that it reflected an inbreeding aristocracy in a class-bound society did not seem to occur to Galton.

There were other problems with his approach, too. For example, Galton almost exclusively looked at men of eminence. One can browse through many pages of his book before encountering the occasional woman, such as Queen Christina of Sweden, "of high ability, but of masculine habits" (206). Napoleon's mother, Letitia Ramolini, is one of the few cases in which a mother is recorded in any eminent man's pedigree, perhaps because Galton considered her "a heroine by nature," as well as being one of the most beautiful women in Corsica (202). Since Galton did not know of Mendel's work, one wonders if he may have believed in the seed model of inheritance, that offspring derived from the male, and the female was the field in which they grew.

Galton's comparison of the "Negro race" with the "Anglo-Saxon race" follows the same general line of thinking and errors as does *The Bell Curve*, which we will examine in a later chapter. For making comparisons like these, there is a fundamental assumption that races as distinct entities exist, a stance we have challenged on a genetic basis. In addition, these comparisons rest on the assumption that complex traits such as eminence or intelligence follow a single number line and that those scores for eminence or intelligence will validly follow a bell-shaped curve. Traits such as weight or height do follow a simple number line: someone weighing 140 pounds is lighter than someone weighing 150 pounds and heavier than someone weighing 130 pounds. If we collect statistics on height or weight for a group of people, we will find that most fall close to the average, with decreasing numbers of people found the further one is above or below the average. The concept of Galton or the authors of *The Bell Curve* is that it is as simple to measure intelligence is as it is to measure weight.

Neither Galton nor the authors of *The Bell Curve* doubted the existence of some eminent blacks, but these authors believe that they are less common than eminent whites, based on the idea that the bell-shaped curve for blacks has a lower average (e.g., Galton, 393–95). What type of data did Galton use to reach this conclusion? He describes how he sought to discuss with any white person he met who had traveled in Africa their impressions of black chiefs, and especially whether the white travelers had felt superior or inferior or equal. Since only a few whites told him that they had been in a situation in which they felt themselves the inferior, Galton considered this reasonable evidence to support a genetic basis for white superiority (Galton, 394–98). He speculated that ultimately, since European colonists had come to Africa, blacks may "in course of time be supplanted and replaced by their betters" (Galton, 40). Galton also drew on various accounts of black slaves in America acting "half-witted" as evidence for white superiority (Galton, 395). As contemporary students of American history know, the African American perspective is that fighting against slavery sometimes meant playing dumb. Galton's own life also tells a story. He had traveled extensively in Africa as a young man, and though many of his letters and papers were destroyed, documentation has survived showing that he purchased an African concubine for himself during his travels; her fate remains unknown (Shipman, 112).

Galton was also one of the prophets of the supermen. He looked to the evolution of a future race as "much superior mentally and morally to the modern European as the modern European is to the lowest of the Negro races" (Galton, 27). Galton later coined the term eugenics (good origin), the concept to improve England, Germany, and the world through selective human breeding.

CONCEPTS OF RACE AND EVOLUTION AMONG OTHER OPINION LEADERS

In the English-speaking world, Spencer popularized these ideas, which came to be called social Darwinism. The American industrialist Andrew Carnegie described his reaction this way:

> That light came in as a flood and all was clear. Not only had I got rid of theology and the supernatural, but I found the truth of evolution. 'All's well since all grows better' . . . We accept and welcome, therefore, as conditions to which we must accommodate ourselves, great inequality of environment; the concentration of business, industrial and commercial, in the hands of a few; the law of competition between these as being not only beneficial, but essential to the future progress of the human race. (Carnegie, quoted in Burke, 271)

In the United States, William Graham Sumner at Yale University was another prominent advocate of social Darwinism. He believed that the unfit and the poor manifest innate inferiority that needed to be evolutionarily eliminated, and natural selection should be allowed to run its course without interference from "meddlers" (Shipman, 110).

Throughout the European and American scientific elite, a racist worldview, bolstered by social Darwinism, was common. In *The Mismeasure of Man,* Gould documents numerous blistering racist quotes from many well-known scientists, such as Georges Cuvier, the great French geologist and comparative anatomist (Gould, 36); Charles Lyell, another founder of geology (36); or Louis Agassiz, famous Swiss naturalist and founder of Harvard's Museum of Comparative Zoology (42–50). T. H. Huxley, Darwin's well-known apologist, wrote,

> No rational man, cognizant of the facts, believes that the average negro is the equal, still less the superior, of the average white man. And, if this be true, it is simply incredible that, when all his disabilities are removed, and our prognathous relative has a fair field and no favor, as well as no oppressor, he will be able to compete successfully with his bigger-brained and smaller-jawed rival, in a contest which is to be carried on by thoughts and not by bites. (quoted in Gould, 71)

In 1908 a Jewish American playwright, Israel Zangwill, had invented a new cliché when he called the United States "the melting pot, where all the races of Europe are melting and reforming" (quoted in Shipman, 123). Even though he left this a strictly European melting pot in his metaphor, this was a threatening concept to those troubled by immigration from new ethnic groups. In 1916 there was an influential response by a man named Madison Grant in *The Passing of the Great Race.* Because the new waves of immigrants were "no longer exclusively members of the Nordic race," Grant felt that there was a need to abandon "altruistic ideals" and "maudlin sentimentalism" toward the oppressed, because the immigrants were otherwise going to push the country into a "racial abyss" (Shipman, 123–24). In Grant's understanding of genetics, it was specifically the mixing of ethnic backgrounds—the melting pot—that would lead to degradation and incompetence, which he felt was surely illustrated by the history and culture of Mexico. That is, he attributed the roots of social problems in Mexico to the fact that the majority of Mexicans are of both Spanish and Indian ancestry.

The American Left was not exempt. Studies have been made, for example, of the many connections between Margaret Sanger and the founding of Planned Parenthood with racial and eugenic ideas (e.g., Grant, 87–104; Marshall and Donovan, 275–89). Upton Sinclair's The Jungle, about stockyard workers in Chicago, advocates for the Socialist Party. However, the few blacks portrayed in its pages seem to be outside the socialist paradise. Most are strikebreakers, along with "the lowest foreigners—Greeks, Romanians, Sicilians and Slovaks" (260). They are described as "a throng of stupid black Negroes" (260); they don't want to work and soon arm themselves (261). Although they are "brawny" (264), they are descended from savages, and "hell was let loose in the yards" (265). To satisfy the black "bucks" (261), the packing companies brought in white prostitutes, along with "young white girls from the country" (265), resulting in a "saturnalia of debauchery —scenes such as never before had been witnessed in America" (265).

All these ideas promoted by intellectuals and scholars became part of Western society, and ideas have consequences wherever they are sown. In the United States, terrorist organizations such as the Ku Klux Klan developed in the 1800s and persist to some degree, with an intentional policy of violence against prominent blacks and against whites who were aiding black community development. The philosophy that blacks constituted a distinct and inferior race, probably morally as well as intellectually, provided an excuse for spontaneous violence. The history of the late 1800s and early 1900s is full of lynchings and burnings of black men by white mobs, who were not particular about establishing guilt or innocence. Letters from that time by recent Swedish immigrants to the American Midwest and West express shock at the way violence in the United States was so casual and injustices to African Americans ignored (e.g., Barton, 195–96; 281–84). For example, a Swede writing from Ironton, Colorado, in 1887 gave eyewitness accounts of a white man who shot another man in cold blood and was soon back on the streets, and a black man who shot a white woman in a fight and was burned alive by a cheering mob, while the police stood back (Barton, 195–96). In eastern Pennsylvania, my children's elementary school does an annual field trip to old homes with secret passages and hidden rooms from the Underground Railroad. Many African American families in eastern Pennsylvania trace their roots to refuge offered them by local white families in the early 1800s. Yet within the same region, events occurred such as the death of Zechariah Walker in Coatesville, Pennsylvania, in 1911. Walker, a black man who may have been guilty of a murder committed while he was drunk, was pulled from a hospital bed by a white mob and burned alive while hundreds cheered (Downey and Hyser).

THE RESPONSE OF CHRISTIANS

While this trend accelerated in intellectual circles, in some evangelical Christian circles there was a sincere effort to oppose bigotry. N. Magnuson, in *Salvation in the Slums: Evangelical Social Work, 1865–1920*, documents in particular the efforts of the Salvation Army and the Christian and Missionary Alliance to be truly multiethnic testimonies of Christ's kingdom. They supported Italian immigrants (Magnuson, 127–30); evangelical Christian orphanages in the South were sometimes firebombed because they were multiracial (124–25); members of the Salvation Army sometimes interposed themselves to try to stop lynchings of blacks (125). The Salvation Army position, summarized in an 1885 editorial, was: "If . . . Negroes lack in any particular the intellect and culture . . . it is not their fault, but their misfortune, caused by the great and wicked selfishness of those who unjustly withhold from them what they abuse them for lacking" (118). They opposed the imposition of the various tests of intelligence for immigrants (128).

The Pentecostal and charismatic movement of the twentieth century also seems to have developed within a general theological matrix that looked beyond the categories of race. An emphasis on seeking a work of grace in addition to salvation developed in close association with John Wesley and other holiness evangelists, especially Charles Grandison Finney, Phoebe Palmer, and D. L. Moody (Dayton). We have already documented how all four of these people were strongly abolitionist and generally opposed to racial segregation. The characteristic most associated with classic Pentecostal doctrine—the gift of tongues as evidence of the baptism of the Holy Spirit—was expressed sporadically at several times and places (e.g., see Christenson, Dayton for reviews of this) in the 1800s and the early 1900s, but it first affected large numbers of people in the event known as the Azusa Street revival, which occurred in Los Angeles in 1906 (e.g., Lovett).

One characteristic of Azusa Street is that it was led by an African American, William J. Seymour, but attracted Americans of all ethnic backgrounds and immigrants of many nationalities. Although Seymour believed in the importance of the gift of tongues, his principal desire was for evangelism of all peoples (e.g., Zimmerman, 12). Seymour intentionally opened the Azusa Street meeting to everyone, defying prevailing racist ideas even in Pentecostal circles (Lovett, 135). Until the 1920s, the Pentecostal movement sustained a great deal of interracial fellowship (e.g., Lovett, 136–39). This broke down during the height of Ku Klux Klan activity: Charles Parham, a white American closely associated with Pentecostal doctrine, even supported the Klan (Lovett, 135). In recent decades, there have been several formal efforts at public forgiveness and reconciliation for sins of racism within the various Pentecostal organizations. The charismatic movement of the last forty years, which has emphasized seeking God's Spirit for the miraculous and brought this to people outside the original Pentecostal denominations, has not had as much baggage. In part, it has been heavily influenced by men such as Dave Wilkerson, who never paid much attention to ethnic boundaries.

Some of the family stories I have received relate directly to this tradition. My mother grew up in a single-parent family in Chicago during the 1920s and 1930s, and they were often very poor. For example, in one apartment that she remembers, her mother would arrange shoes in a row next to her bed, so they were ready to throw at the rats during the night. When she was not quite a teen, my mother became the first evangelical Christian in her extended family, through the influence of a small Scottish Covenanter church in her neighborhood. They shared a storefront with an African American church. The Scottish Covenanter denomination sings the versified psalms a cappella: my mother vividly remembers how members of the black church would come early to their service to join in the Covenanter service, adding beautiful, rich harmonies to the old a cappella melodies. College was out of the question, but as an adult my mother was able to afford night classes at the Moody Bible Institute. These classes were always multiracial and multiethnic; that was understood to be the biblical way, consistent with the abolitionist views of its founder, D. L. Moody. While she was a part-time student there, a women's choir from the Moody Bible Institute toured the South. Black members, including the pianist, were refused service in a restaurant, so the entire choir stood and left.

My mother also vividly remembers a black preacher, Mr. Lilly, who was a popular speaker at white Bible churches in the Chicago area, and a close friend of the (white) man who introduced my parents to each other. Mr. Lilly was a chaplain at the public hospitals, where he would share from the Bible and pray with patients, black or white, and also provide kits for personal hygiene to forgotten people. This latter ministry had developed from an occasion when he thought he heard a dog coming down the hall of the veteran's hospital, but it proved to be a neglected man who had had no one to trim his toenails, and his nails clicked on the linoleum floor like a dog's. Mr. Lilly would trim nails for people who were unable to do so for themselves.

These seem like small things six and seven decades later, but this was at a time when white supremacist groups like the Ku Klux Klan were at the height of their power and black people were not safe merely walking through many of the white ethnic neighborhoods in Chicago. Why did the people who most honored the Bible not speak up more against racism? Many of these Christians were, I think, themselves quite poor in the Depression, and furthermore considered themselves as besieged by the opinion leaders of society and the college-educated. They were to a large degree labeled fundamentalists and their perspective dismissed. A strongly dispensationalist theology, emphasizing personal holiness in preparation for Jesus' return and discouraging political or academic vocations for Christians in a society destined only to ever greater corruption also worked against addressing racism in society, even for those most just in their personal lives. How we wish now that they had preached more boldly the whole counsel of God, including God creating from one blood all nations (Acts 18:26). But we can now only be responsible for our actions, how we now faithfully speak all of God's truth to our generation.

WHAT ABOUT EVOLUTION?

My perspective on the issue of whether or to what degree evolution has occurred is based on the high view of God's authority as Creator and Sovereign that we encounter throughout the Bible. There is not a gap in the Bible between God's action in the natural world, described by the word *providence,* and through miracles, events that do not follow cause and effect as we are able to measure it. That is, God is not limited to the miraculous; there is no place in the universe that is not before the presence of God, not even the simplest chemical reactions or humblest prayers. There is no essential conflict between God creating the world we encounter today using evolutionary processes or using miracles or some combination of both that we cannot imagine. The first three chapters of Genesis are written in a highly stylized, poetic form, a context that suggests that they summarize the truth of God as Creator but not in a manner that we should read as scientific prose. An excellent book for further reading on this subject is *In the Beginning,* by an evangelical French theologian, Henrí Blocher (1984).

However, there is a conflict between Christians and some members of the scientific community who hold to a doctrinaire empiricism—the worldview that only what can be perceived with the senses is real—over the nature of humanity being spiritual as well as physical. This is knowledge gained by revelation—God revealing what we could not discover by experimentation or logic alone—and it cannot be proved empirically.

An irony as one reads through the literature from the mid-1800s to the mid-1900s is the recognition that the most racist apologetics, robed in scientific language, were coming from institutions founded as Christian colleges, such as Harvard, Yale, or Princeton. In the late 1800s and early 1900s there is evidence that many liberal Christians, believing they were embracing science, embraced an imperialistic bigotry even while the most activist evangelical Christians, rejecting the prevailing bigotry built upon an evolutionary apologetic, simultaneously turned away from serious consideration of science. The original context of these choices was later forgotten, and they took on a cultural life of their own.

Thus the concept of a superior white race and an inferior black race—and probably other races as well—became part of the worldview of most white Americans. But what was it that was different? How could one identify race reliably?

CHAPTER 8

■

The Scientific Community and the Concept of Racial Superiority

T HE PROBLEM FOR THOSE WHO BELIEVE IN THE EXISTENCE OF races, and particularly the superiority of one over another, is to show that real differences exist that can be demonstrated objectively. Which differences were important seems to vary from culture to culture. In Latin America, the white Castilian aristocracy's preoccupation with bloodlines is reflected in the terms *mestizo,* referring to someone of Spanish-Indian ancestry, and *mulato,* referring to someone of Spanish-African ancestry. In North America, there has not been a strong bias against Native American ancestry. Media personalities such as Will Rogers, Oral Roberts, or Cher probably never faced discrimination because they were or are of mostly Native American blood. Nor did having the ancestry of Pocahontas hurt the careers of Thomas Jefferson or Robert E. Lee, whereas had they shared a black ancestor, their lives would have been quite different.

Large numbers of North Americans have some Indian blood, and generally it's a point of family pride. In contrast, in many Latin American countries there remains prejudice against the Indian face, although it has been less of a barrier in some families than others and less important everywhere in recent years. I once met a woman from Guatemala, where the vast majority of the people are either Native American or *mestizo.* Even while living in rural areas within this country for centuries, her family has kept "pure" Spanish bloodlines, sometimes by cousins marrying cousins rather than marrying an Indian or a *mestizo.* (She married a friend of mine, who is *mestizo:* to her, the issue is irrelevant, particularly since she and her husband are evangelical Christians.) In North America, however, there has been much greater preoccupation with the color of the skin than with the form of the countenance. All of this may be reflected by the adoption into commonly used American English of the Spanish words *negro* and *mulato,* but not *mestizo.*

THE BIOLOGY OF SKIN COLOR

The problem with skin color, of course, is it's only skin deep! Color differences from black to white are caused by varying amounts of melanin, a chemical that blocks ultraviolet light. Tanning, which is short-term production of extra melanin, is a defensive reaction of the skin to exposure to the ultraviolet radiation present in sunlight, which damages chromosomes in the skin cells and increases risk of skin cancer. There is a long-standing estimate of four to five genes, each with two additive alleles, involved in the human inheritance of levels of melanin. That is, there are believed to be at least nine to eleven discernible levels of pigmentation possible in the grandchildren of black-white marriages (e.g., Cummings, 356–59; Stern). There is an advantage to blocking most of the ultraviolet light in tropical areas, since this protects against skin cancer, but there is a disadvantage in areas with less sunlight and long winters, since some ultraviolet light is necessary to make vitamin D, without which children develop rickets, or lack of bone development.

Although the most dramatic differences in the degree of melanin lie along the north-south gradient of skin pigmentation from west central Africa to northern Europe, there are also pigmentation gradients among the original peoples of Asia and the Americas (e.g., Kottak, 83–86), indicating that this is a common evolutionary change that occurs in the human race. Human skin color also varies in red and pink hues by how close an individual's capillaries are to the surface and in yellow and golden hues by how close to the skin surface fatty insulation is placed, but estimates of the genes involved in these differences have never been attempted.

If there are races that are profoundly different from each other in abilities and motivations, then there must be some way to easily tell them apart. By the 1800s skin color itself was well-known to be a trait subject to great variation, although in English-speaking cultures, especially the United States, there developed what has been called the one-drop rule. In this concept, even a tiny amount of African ancestry could categorize a person as black. A specialized terminology grew up in the English-speaking Caribbean and United States around various dilutions of African blood (e.g., Olby, 68). The hypocrisy of the antebellum South between the theory of diverse racial subspecies and everyday reality was highlighted by abolitionist William Lloyd Garrison (Frederickson 1968, 35):

Nature, we are positively assured, has raised up impassable barriers between the races. I understand by this expression, that the blacks are of a different species from ourselves, so that all attempts to generate offspring between us and them must prove as abortive, as between a man and a beast. . . . Now the planters at the south have clearly demonstrated that an amalgamation with their slaves is not only possible, but a matter of course, and eminently productive. . . . In truth, it is often so difficult in the slave States to distinguish between the fruits of this intercourse and the children of white parents, that witnesses are summoned at court to solve the problem! . . . Happy indeed would it be for many a female slave, if such a barrier could exist during the period of her servitude to protect her from the lust of her master!

In Virginia, in the early 1900s, 1/16 African ancestry established a person as a Negro; in Louisiana in the 1970s, the state legislature was debating whether the line for racial classification as a Negro should be drawn at 1/64 or 1/32 African ancestry (Allen, 27–28). This issue arose because a woman who had always believed herself white discovered in middle age that the state of Louisiana categorized her in official documents as "colored" (Kottak, 77).

In the Dominican Republic the same concept developed, but it turned inside out. The country was a slave-based economy for centuries, and the Haitians, the first predominantly black republic in the world, controlled it from 1822 to 1844. The black Haitians generated enormous animosity among the lighter-skinned Dominicans during this occupation, but the Dominicans were also developing as a people in which the majority have some African ancestry. Later, from 1930 until his assassination in 1961, Rafael Trujillo ruled the country as a Caribbean-style fascist dictator. Although Trujillo was mulato (of mixed black and white ancestry), he emphasized Hispanidad—Hispanicity, based on traditional Spanish culture —and forged close ties with Francisco Franco in Spain. He inflamed the traditional animosity toward black Haitians and on one occasion in 1937 organized the deaths of between twelve thousand and twenty-five thousand Haitian laborers in a single night. In a society where most of the population has at least some African ancestry but white ancestry is more valued, the one-drop concept developed in reference to white rather than black ancestry.

Even a small amount of European ancestry traditionally made one something other than black. In 1998 I encountered a newspaper article surveying seventeen terms by which Dominicans described their own skin color. The largest percentage (46%) of respondents defined their skin color as Indian (i.e., brown; Mieses). Dominican friends emphasized to me that the terms were also a sort of euphemistic courtesy within a racist system, to seek to refer to someone as anything but black—like a Haitian. Dominicans have sometimes experienced culture shock in their travels to the United States: in the Dominican Republic they had thought of themselves as white or Indian, but in the United States they were treated as blacks.

These examples document that the preoccupation with race implies that there is something deeper than just skin color, that there is something profoundly different in African ancestry. But if so, what was it?

"RACE" AS A CATEGORY IN FORENSICS

In 1997–1998 the American Anthropological Association made the topic of race the theme for its monthly *Anthropology Newsletter*. For readers interested in additional background, these issues contain a wealth of useful information and debate. One important reservation that was raised about scrapping the concept of race has to do with forensics, the study of human remains, especially in police work. George W. Gill of the University of Wyoming teaches and researches forensic techniques, and he defended racial categories, provided their limitations are kept in mind, for identifying skeletal remains (Gill). His article includes graphed examples of measurement data for bones of the nose and eye region, or the femur (the thigh bone). Gill reports it is possible to correctly identify an unknown skeleton about 85% of the time as being from a white, black, or Native American person, if enough measurements are taken. Note that this also means there is 15% overlap (or more) among categories of race. Gill understands these race categories as being within the framework of human genetic variation, of populations differing in a number of physical measurements, but nothing as distinct as subspecies. This article does not address people from multiethnic backgrounds, who would be expected to fall between categories. For example, forensic study of ancient Egyptian remains revealed a range of head patterns for "European" to "sub-Saharan African" with many intermediate types: a "multiracial" people (Ortíz de Montellano, 34–35).

THE SEARCH FOR THE RACIAL FRONTIER: INTELLIGENCE

The classic book on the history of the search for racial differences is *The Mismeasure of Man,* by Stephen Jay Gould. There was a long search for a single trait, besides skin color, associated with intelligence and social potential. Such a trait could be easily followed, ideally, on some sort of linear scale, permitting ranking. In many cases Gould was able to review original data, and he demonstrates the errors in the work of the scientists used as bulwarks of racial superiority, among them Samuel George Morton, Paul Broca, and the entire industry that grew up around intelligence quotient (IQ).

Skull Volume

Samuel George Morton (1799–1851) was a Philadelphia scientist and doctor who collected skulls from many ethnic groups and measured skull volume by filling skulls with rice grains or lead shot. Morton attempted to show that skull volume, and therefore intelligence, was greatest in the white race in general and the English in particular (e.g., Gould, 54–55). Gould has assembled evidence that Morton manipulated data categories to accomplish this. For example, Morton combined the skull volume data from the relatively small-bodied Quechua people of the Inca Empire in Peru with those of the large-bodied Sioux or Lakota people from the North American Great Plains, producing a Native American skull volume average lower than that of northern Europeans; data for the skull volumes of the Sioux surpassed that of most Europeans (Gould, 56–57). From Morton's own lab notebooks, Gould demonstrated that the skull volumes of Negroes were consistently undermeasured in his early work, when he later checked the accuracy of his measurements with seed by using lead shot to remeasure the same set of skulls. Hence, there was a conscious or unconscious bias (Gould, 64–67). Morton also did not separate by sex: men, on average, have bigger skulls than do women. All of his samples of superior races were predominantly male; in the case of his English sample, there were all male skulls (68), resulting in the largest average volume and hence alleged English superiority.

Although Morton's hypothesis—that skull volume indicated intelligence—was eventually disproved by various data, including the rather obvious observation that small men with small skulls, such as Napoleon or the Quechua people, are not limited in intelligence, Morton's conclusions lived on as justifications for various policies. His books were one of the arguments used in the South in opposition to abolitionists. *The Charleston Medical Journal,* for example, eulogized him, saying, "We of the South should consider him as our benefactor, for aiding most materially in giving to the negro his true position as an inferior race" (quoted in Gould, 69).

BRAIN SIZE

Paul Broca (1824–1880) was a renowned professor of medicine influential in the development of modern neuroscience, as well as participating in founding the Anthropological Society of Paris. Since skull volume had proved useless, Broca developed various measures for intelligence and/or criminality based on brain size and/or size and ratio of parts of the brain. His studies in part were based on the voluntary donation of their brains by European men of eminence to be compared with the brains of criminals and men of other races, as well as with female brains, mostly European (Gould, 82–107). He was frank about his methods: "We surmount the problem easily by choosing for our comparison of brains, races whose intellectual inequalities are completely clear. Thus the superiority of Europeans compared with African Negroes, American Indians . . . is sufficiently certain to serve as a point of departure for the comparison of brains" (quoted in Gould, 88).

There were numerous uncontrolled variables in Broca's work, which Gould discusses at length. How much of the spinal cord should be left attached, for example, before measuring a brain? How long after death was the brain removed? How much of the membranes surrounding the brain, or the preservatives keeping the brain from decaying, were included in a weight? In addition, Broca kept encountering individuals who didn't fit his model, such as large-brained criminals and small-brained men of eminence. Broca did demonstrate a consistent average difference in male and female brains, which he used to argue against women's suffrage (Gould, 103–6). One of his colleagues, Gustave Le Bon, a founder of social psychology, wrote, "In the most intelligent races, as among the Parisians, there are a huge number of women whose brains are closer in size to those of gorillas than to the most developed male brains. The inferiority is so obvious that no one can contest it for a moment" (quoted in Gould, 104).

Because of these problems and for additional reasons, brain size, head shape, or other physical traits were largely discarded by scientists by the twentieth century as being valid measures of intelligence. Rather than abandon the futile quest for a simple way to categorize people, scientists sought to fill the social need to separate people into groups of the superior and the inferior by intelligence tests, especially the intelligence quotient (IQ). Science was advancing during this time by the discovery that many natural phenomena follow the normal distribution, or the bell-shaped curve, and by the discovery of Mendelian genetics. This provided a new tangent to explore to compare racial differences.

INTELLIGENCE QUOTIENT

One reason Mendel is thought to have not been understandable to his generation was his mathematical approach to a biological question. By the time of Mendel's rediscovery in 1900, the usefulness of quantitative analysis in biology, rather than just prose description, was being widely discovered. Simultaneously, Mendel's principles were being shown to apply to inheritance of many qualitative traits in living things, that is, traits with distinct physical differences, such as black fur versus white fur. The power of genetics in granting new understanding was impressive, but there was an enormous, subtle pressure to find ways to put numbers on traits that to that point had not been measurable on a number line.

In the early 1900s, Alfred Binet, a French educator at the Sorbonne, developed a test, based on the French school curriculum, to identify children behind their grade level who could use extra help. This was based on the observation that all children do not master the same skills at the same age, and it was never intended to rank intelligence per se. When multiplied by 100, the score became a whole number, later called, in the United States, the Intelligence Quotient, or IQ.

$$IQ = \frac{\text{Age level at which child performed (rel. to all French children)}}{\text{Actual age of child X 100}}$$

Since American children tested lower than did French children on the test, Lewis Terman of Stanford University developed the Stanford-Binet IQ, based on curriculum in the United States. At this point, in the United States at least, the IQ took on a life of its own, still reflected in the use of "IQ" as a synonym for intelligence in American English. Gould devotes a large portion of his book to this issue (155–233), and we will review the work of several men that he gives attention to, as well as additional examples of the use of IQ and related tests to confirm social rankings.

Henry Goddard was research director at the Vineland School for the Feeble-minded in Vineland, New Jersey. He was a leading advocate of the isolation and/or sterilization of the feeble-minded (as measured by IQ tests) as a means to save the integrity of American society. Some of the American laws that developed from this effort were later used as the templates of similar laws in Nazi Germany. Goddard was convinced that the feeble-minded, for whom he coined the term morons, were the way they were because of a single Mendelian gene (Gould, 162–63); hence, the trait potentially could be eliminated in one to two generations. At the invitation of the U.S. Public Health Service, by 1913 Goddard was beginning to study immigrants at Ellis Island. His results, published in the refereed Journal of Delinquency, concluded that 83% of Jews, 80% of Hungarians, 79% of Italians, and 87% of Russian immigrants were morons (Gould, 166). In this intellectual climate, large changes were made in immigration laws in the early 1920s that essentially ended large-scale immigration from eastern and southern Europe. Duster (1990, 9–14) points out how the low test scores by Jewish immigrants prior to World War I were at that time assumed to be due to genetic factors, but the higher-than-average scores of contemporary Jewish Americans are now assumed to be due to cultural factors. That is, genetically inferior Jews were an acceptable concept; genetically superior Jews are not.

During World War I, massive IQ testing of more than a million men was done under the leadership of Goddard, Terman, Robert Yerkes of Harvard, and Carl Brigham of Princeton University. Among their conclusions, reported to the U.S. Congress after the war, was that the average mental age of these men, all over eighteen, was about thirteen. (If such a statistic as "mental age" exists, the average mental age of a million men over eighteen must, by definition, be over eighteen.) They also concluded that the United States faced genetic peril from Italian immigrants, whose average mental age was eleven by the tests, and American Negroes, whose average mental age was ten (Gould, 197). The fact that the average scores of blacks from four Northern states were higher than the average scores of whites from nine Southern states troubled the researchers, although some suggested that the smartest blacks had gone north (217–18). Brigham, who later helped develop the Scholastic Aptitude test (SAT), concluded, "These army data constitute the first really significant contribution to the study of race differences in mental traits. They give us a scientific basis for our conclusions" (quoted in Gould, 224). In an influential book (1923), Brigham concluded that science had demonstrated the genetic superiority of Germanic peoples, but that superior heritage was at risk:

> The decline of American intelligence will be more rapid than the decline of the intelligence of European national groups, owing to the presence here of the negro. These are the plain, if somewhat ugly, facts that our study shows. The deterioration of American intelligence is not inevitable, however, if public action can be aroused to prevent it. There is not reason why legal steps should not be taken which would insure a continuously progressive upward evolution.
>
> The steps that should be taken . . . must of course be dictated by science. . . . Immigration should not only be restrictive, but highly selective. . . . The really important steps are those looking toward the prevention of the continued propagation of defective strains in the present population. (Brigham, quoted in Gould, 230)

Henry Fairfield Osborn, president of the American Museum of Natural History, spoke of Brigham's results this way:

> We have learned once and for all that the negro is not like us. So in regard to many races and subraces in Europe we learned that some which we had believed possessed of an order of intelligence perhaps superior to ours were in fact far inferior. (quoted in Gould, 231)

IMMIGRATION, INTELLIGENCE, AND EUGENICS

This type of thinking was not restricted to a few scientists. Let us look at the attitude toward southern European immigrants in *Applied Eugenics* (Poponoe and Johnson), published in 1920. Both authors were scientific opinion leaders: Paul Poponoe was then editor of the well-known scientific journal, the *Journal of Heredity;* R. H. Johnson, a professor of petroleum geology at the University of Pittsburgh, also published extensively on eugenics and evolution. They openly express concern about the "new arrivals," for they may be "races which are biologically more or less distinct" (300), which may result in "the evil of crossbreeding" (301). In addition, the southern and eastern Europeans who come are inferior genetic samples even from among their own people; they are "vigorous, ignorant peasants" (302). Latent genetic weaknesses may manifest themselves after immersion in the modern industrial world of the United States: "The mental weakness appears only after he has been here some years . . . perhaps because he finds his environment in, say, lower Manhattan Island so much more taxing to the brain than the simple surroundings of his farm overlooking the bay of Naples" (303). A "falling off in the frequency of good looks in the American people" is expected because of the new arrivals (301). In addition, they are concerned that immigrants such as the Italians will interbreed or intermarry with American blacks, because the "taboo is weak" (296).

In 1924 the Immigration Restriction Act was passed, creating very low quotas for all the eastern and southern European countries—and Jews. Calvin Coolidge said, when he signed the bill, "America must be kept American" (Duster 1990, 12), and this bill was an important reason Jewish refugees were later unable to come to the United States from Nazi-occupied Europe. These laws both reflected and perpetuated a climate of prejudice. My late Italian American mother-in-law, for example, had vivid childhood memories of rocks being thrown through her family's windows in Pennsylvania because there was jealousy when her immigrant father's mushroom business began to prosper. She also recounted experiences as a teenager evading the regulations in resort towns on the Jersey shore that prohibited blacks, Jews, and Italians from being in the town limits after sunset.

A more sinister example is Charles Dight, who through the 1930s was an activist on behalf of genetic laws in the United States, as well as involved in establishing prizes at the Minnesota State Fair for the most genetically fit families. Dight, who served as a professor in the University of Minnesota Medical School and later as a Socialist alderman in Minneapolis, in 1933 sent Hitler a copy of an article he had written, "praising your plan to stamp out mental inferiority among the German people" and hoping it "will advance the eugenics movement in other nations as well as Germany" (Kizilos). (Dight was not a professor at the University of Minnesota when he wrote this letter.) As president of the Minnesota Eugenics Society, Dight presented Charles Lindbergh with a plaque "in recognition of his superior hereditary endowment" with the subtitle, "Eugenics may redeem mankind" (Kizilos).

In a college textbook from 1936, *Human Genetics and Its Social Import,* S. J. Holmes, a zoology professor at the University of California, begins his discussion of "Race Betterment" with the Greeks: the Spartans, then Plato's *Republic,* and Aristotle's *Politics* (360–61), then moves to Darwin and the application of Darwinian evolution to human society. "Eugenics societies," he writes, "have been formed in many countries, Norway, Sweden, France . . . and especially Germany where there now is an active and widespread interest in eugenic reform" (Holmes, 364). Holmes praised involuntary sterilization of "defectives," noting how such a Virginia statute was upheld by the U.S. Supreme Court, with Justice Oliver Wendell Holmes pronouncing, "three generations of imbeciles are enough" (Holmes, 371). He noted that there has been some opposition "on religious grounds, especially by adherents of the Roman Catholic church" (372), but he gives little detail. He noted, "the largest number of operations have been carried out in Germany under the recent sterilization law" (373), twice the number done that year in these United States, on "persons adjudged to be hereditarily defective by the [German] High Court of Eugenics" (374). Throughout this textbook, the eugenics of Nazi Germany is favorably compared with that of the United States: they are seen as variations of a common theme. By 1935 genetic marriage counseling, including prohibitions of marriage outside ethnic lines, was obligatory in Germany; people who married in defiance of a eugenic decision faced imprisonment (Shipman, 137).

Terman, who developed the Standford-Binet IQ tests, tested thousands of children in California and identified 1,444 between eight and twelve as geniuses (IQs of 140 to 200). The "Termites," as they were known to researchers, were followed throughout their lives (for some, the study is ongoing). Students were chosen for inclusion partly based on IQ tests and partly on teacher assessment of the brightest students (Shurkin, 31–33). Schools for delinquents were passed over, since it was assumed the children were less bright or they wouldn't be there (Shurkin, 33). The majority of the students were of Anglo-Saxon ancestry, with greater percentages of Jews than the general population, and tiny percentages of Mexican Americans or blacks (Terman et al., 55; Shurkin, 39). Terman and his associates at Stanford lumped together children of Italian, Portuguese, and Mexican ancestry in a category called Latin. For the Latins, "consistently low scores" were reported, with a median IQ of 80 as a "liberal estimate," and the researchers hinted that the "true causes lie deeper than the environment" (Terman et al., 57).

The perspective of sixty years has yielded some unexpected results from Terman's work. For example, partial follow-up of children tested and rejected as merely average in these studies revealed the Nobel Laureates Luis Alvaréz and William Shockley; in contrast, no Termites won a Nobel Prize, although some did make the National Academy of Sciences (Shurkin, 35). Those persons with the high IQs have also retrospectively been divided into those who had happier, more successful lives and those who did not, and a variety of home life differences between these groups have been shown to exist (Shurkin, 280). Nurture was important, after all.

STATISTICAL ISSUES WITH INDEX VALUES

When complex traits such as intelligence are reduced to a single number line —a set of measurements in a row (such as inch marks on a ruler)—there are serious statistical problems. A common problem that can deceive any researcher and often confuses the general public is that all numbers are not alike in terms of what kind of statistical analysis can be used. That is, different types of measurements cannot all be analyzed validly in the same way.

Not All Numbers Are Equal

The strongest type of numbers for producing reliable statistical analysis are based on what is called *ratio levels of measurement*. This refers to a direct relationship with physical reality. Weight is a ratio level measure; if nothing is on a scale, the measurement is zero, and a two-hundred-pound man weighs exactly twice as much as a one-hundred-pound man. *Interval level measures* is the term used for numbers that also have a direct relationship to physical realities, but with a slightly more artificial scale. There is an unchanging interval between points on the scale used, but the numbers are arbitrary. Temperature scales are the classic example of interval level measures. A temperature of zero does not mean there is no temperature, but the interval between 10 and 20 degrees is the same as that between 210 and 220 degrees.

Many numbers generated in the social sciences and economics are not ratio or interval data but belong to one of the other two categories commonly recognized. Ordinal level measures are numbers derived, it is hoped, from objective reality, but the measures are indirect and often are *index values*, which we shall examine in more detail shortly. Ordinal numbers follow a number line that permits ranking of scores, but the intervals between numbers are not necessarily constant the way interval numbers are, and different scores are not necessarily measuring the same thing. School grades are an ordinal system: the difference between an A and a B is not necessarily the same thing, in terms of real understanding of a subject, as that between a C and a D.

Finally, *nominal level measures* merely assign numbers arbitrarily to categories. If we were studying human eye color, we could place brown-eyed people in Group 1 and blue-eyed in Group 2, or vice versa; the numbers would be arbitrary. It is assumed in a nominal numbering system developed for analysis of differences among the numbered categories that distinct differences really exist. Sometimes this is true: human eyes can more or less be categorized nominally as brown, blue, and some other colors, although even in this case there are enough shade differences that it is not as simple as it sounds. However, studies claiming analysis of intelligence differences among the races, as well as discussions of proposed gay genes or criminal genes, all assume nominal categories that may not exist as distinct entities. This author contends that human nature often best follows a multidimensional continuum rather than distinct categories.

Public opinion polls are another example of nominal analysis. The pollee is expected to choose only from among the options the pollster offers. The only time I have ever been polled, it was a frustrating experience for this very reason. In each question, I was given several choices regarding aspects of United States involvement in a Latin American country. In this case, I had traveled in the region, knew citizens from that nation, and had read several books about the history of the problem. To me it was a situation with many ambiguities, and each of the pollster's nominal categories involved oversimplifications. When I tried to provide a different, more qualified answer to each question, the pollster would finally say, "Well, I'll put you down again under 'no opinion,'" which was not accurate at all.

Index Values Have Many Ingredients

In studies of the genetics of human behavior or intelligence, one common error has been to create *index values,* which are ordinal data, and then work with them as though they were ratio or interval data. An index value is a single number that summarizes in some way a series of other numbers. As a teacher, I regularly work with index values in the form of test scores and course grades. I must choose a set of questions that I hope sample fairly the course material I covered. Different types of questions (multiple choice, essay, etc.) are often mixed in varying proportions, depending on a teacher's preferences. The test scores are thus index values of these sample questions, affected by what the professor stressed or did not stress during those particular class sessions and the questions chosen to represent the content of lectures and labs.

Course grades are yet more complex index values, constructed from several exams, term papers, and other assignments. The teacher has to choose what he or she believes is a reliable combination—should that term paper count for 10% or 20% of the grade? Over an entire academic program, the GPA or grade point average is thus an index of indices of indices and subject to numerous currents and prevailing winds. College students at most schools, for example, are well aware of the meaninglessness of high grades in certain majors, whereas in a different major, hard work may be needed to earn a C, for which the recipient is then grateful. And as all college professors know, grades are often not strong predictors of whether a student achieves success in life or career. The most complex index values of all, such as the Consumer Price Index (CPI) or per capita Gross National Product (GNP), are used in economic analysis—and the components of their construction and how they should be analyzed and interpreted remain sharp issues of contention among policy makers.

Index Values Not Accurate for Ranking Things

Because of the errors inherent in ranking index values, they serve best when they are used only to set a threshold. Some minimum SAT score for entrance to a college, for example, is thought to help identify those students with little chance of success in college-level courses *at that moment in their lives:* the low score could be due to lack of natural abilities, or it could be due to a lack of educational opportunities or preparation up to that point. Likewise, students with very high SAT scores probably have abilities and/or an educational background that has prepared them for difficult college programs, but there is little real information gained by attempting to rank a group of incoming college honors students by scores like the SAT. The practice of ranking of people by index values like IQs or SATs, or even ranking of countries by statistics like per capita GNP, is full of errors.

Consider then the concept of the IQ: first, a set of questions must be chosen that somehow represents sample challenges intelligence can solve. The sum of scores for all the questions is then divided by the average score for individuals of that age, although we know that children of the same age often differ greatly in life experience, and multiplied by 100. (Versions developed for adults do not divide by an age factor.) Thus IQ is an index of other numbers. In many, perhaps most, test systems, the scores are then standardized to artificially fit a normal curve distribution for ease of interpretation. The step of fitting the scores to a normal curve requires the assumption that the average score is truly representative of average intelligence in the society at large. Intelligence, whatever all it may encompass in reality, was reduced in the minds of eugenicists such as Terman or Goddard to a single number that could be treated as though it were physical data—like the weights of sacks of potatoes—when in fact they were running statistics on statistics about something that can't be directly observed. And those statistics themselves were changing as society changed.

The questions chosen, no matter how carefully, often have hidden ambiguities or assumptions of previous experience, as Gould demonstrates at length for the IQ tests used by the U.S. Army and the Immigration and Naturalization Service earlier in the twentieth century (199–222). As we will discuss later in the chapter, IQ and related scores have been increasing in most industrialized countries during the twentieth century, sometimes very dramatically within the past two generations (e.g., Flynn). The change has been most pronounced in nonverbal and therefore supposedly culturally independent tests; simultaneously, at least in the United States, verbal SAT scores are dropping, suggesting decreased language skills (e.g., Greenfield). P. M. Greenfield discusses various subtle influences, such as increased reliance on visual images via television and video rather than the written word, that are a part of a child's real education and prepare contemporary children to answer the types of questions the IQ tests ask. The test known as Raven Progressive Matrices, for example, requires discernment of relations among "a series of meaningless figures" and keeping track of several such series at the same time (e.g., Flynn, esp. 9–10). Video games often involve just that. Those that require mental rotating of perspective may be especially effective training to get high scores on tests that involve similar problems with geometric figures, thus making them not quite as culture-free as originally thought (Greenfield).

There are other forces at work, too, besides the construction and content of questions, in any attempt to place a value on an individual's genetic capability for intelligence. Nutrition of all kinds and at all stages of life—prenatal; whether a baby is breastfed or not; calories in the diet; protein content and quality; vitamins; iron—as well as access to clean water and good health care, have almost certainly affected average achievements on tests (e.g., Sigman and Whaley; Martorell; Lynn). As J. U. Ogbu has stressed, all intelligence or personality tests measure the phenotype of an individual: that which is expressed to the world as the product of all genetic inheritance, all environmental influences: physical, such as nutrition, as well as social, personal volition, and, I would add as a Christian, spiritual influences. We can never directly measure the genotype—the actual genetic potential—for intelligence.

IQ STILL USED TO BOLSTER RACIAL THEORIES

Although the eugenicists, and even the word eugenics, almost disappeared as the death camps were fully revealed in Nazi Europe, the concept of racial differences has not died, as illustrated by *The Bell Curve* (Herrnstein and Murray), published in 1994. One of the problems in this book is that the authors continue to treat IQ scores as though they were physical data from human populations: their data really exist (that is, they did not make up the studies), but the analyses violate principles covered in any introductory statistics course. The assumption of a single score representing intelligence that follows mathematical rules for a single, normally distributed variable is stated frankly near the beginning of the book:

> We have said that we will be drawing most heavily on data from the classical tradition. That implies that we also accept certain conclusions undergirding that tradition. . . . Here are six conclusions regarding tests of cognitive ability, drawn from the classical tradition, that are by now beyond significant technical dispute:
>
> 1. There is such a thing as a general factor of cognitive ability on which human beings differ.
> 2. . . . IQ tests expressly designed for that purpose measure it most accurately.
> 3. IQ scores match, to a first degree, whatever it is that people mean when they use the word intelligent or smart in ordinary language.

4. IQ scores are stable . . . over much of a person's life.
5. Properly administered IQ tests are not demonstrably biased against social, economic, ethnic or racial groups.
6. Cognitive ability is substantially heritable . . . (Herrnstein and Murray, 22–23)

Regardless of what Herrnstein and Murray say, these are mostly assumption rather than conclusion, and they are indeed disputed on technical grounds. What they call "classical studies," others would call "old studies" or "outdated studies." As Gould points out (232–33), some of the most prominent early advocates of IQ as a single, stable measure of intelligence by which to rank Americans, or create nominal categories of morons and imbeciles, later rejected their earlier statements as evidence accumulated about the unreliability of IQ. Why then do Herrnstein and Murray want to return to draw "most heavily on data from the classical tradition"?

Samples of The Bell Curve

A sampling of the authors' arguments may inform us. Chapter 15 of *The Bell Curve* (341–68) concerns "the demography of intelligence," which in this case focuses on what they call "dysgenic pressure on IQ." "Dysgenic" is derived from Greek word roots to indicate bad origins or ill origins, in the way that "dysfunctional family" means an ill-functioning or badly functioning family. They note the bad name the word eugenics received by Nazism and its "perversion of eugenics"(343). However, they then proceed to debate whether national intelligence, for genetic reasons, has been dropping consistently for more than a century, or only intermittently dropping. That it has been dropping, they do not seem to doubt. They believe the United States is at risk for two reasons—the unchecked flow of immigrants and the tendency of the poorest and least intelligent to reproduce at faster rates than do the "cognitive elite" (their term throughout the book). Unlike eugenicists of earlier generations, the authors do not mention Italian or Russian Jewish immigrants as one of the "dysgenic" perils, but a great deal of attention is paid to differences among "blacks," "whites," and "Latinos," with membership in each of these groups poorly defined. Based on "shifting ethnic makeup . . . given the differing intrinsic birth rates of the various ethnic groups," Herrnstein and Murray calculate a "dysgenic effect" of about 0.8 IQ point or more per generation (347). That means that after 120 generations, the average IQ would be 0.

The Bell Curve's Central Idea

In the chapter "central to the larger themes of the book" (299), Herrnstein and Murray marshal their data to conclude "one standard deviation (15 IQ points) separates American blacks and whites . . . we assume that IQ is 60 percent heritable" (298). Although they grant that there will be blacks who will be part of the cognitive elite, "given the cognitive differences among ethnic and racial groups, the cognitive elite cannot represent all groups equally" (315).

These themes are carried on throughout 845 pages, but a central problem remains unresolved. The authors assume that human intelligence can be reduced to a single index score, which can then be treated as though it were a physical reality such as a person's weight. As we noted, index constructs such as the IQ or the SAT might be used to set a lower threshold for evaluating an applicant's admission to a college at a particular moment, but analysis that requires ranking of all scores and comparison of the overlapping of bell curves from different populations, such as Herrnstein and Murray do, has serious statistical problems. Investigative reporting (Samuel) revealed that Herrnstein and Murray, as well as many of the researchers they liberally quote, were funded by the Pioneer Fund, a granting agency founded in 1937 "to conduct or aid in conducting study and research into the problem of heredity and eugenics in the human race generally . . . and study into problems of human race betterment with special reference to the people of the United States." Until 1985, that charter statement read "white" in place of "human" (Samuel).

ALTERNATIVES TO MEASURING INTELLIGENCE ON A NUMBER LINE

The Flynn Effect

James R. Flynn, an American who is at the University of Otago, New Zealand, has demonstrated another serious problem with the use of IQ tests to categorize human potential by ethnic origin: IQ and related test scores have been rising all over the industrialized world for decades. Especially in controlled settings, such as countries with universal military service for men, in which the same tests have been given since World War II, the average scores keep increasing. This has required periodic readjustment upward of the IQ value of 100 to higher test scores. It is possible to take IQ test scores from earlier in the century and calculate a contemporary IQ value from them. This produces remarkable results, such as the average IQ of Dutch soldiers being 79 in 1952 relative to the IQ standard of 100 derived in 1982 (Flynn, 33). If, however, the 1952 scores should be the standard, that would result in about 1 in 10 Dutch currently having IQ scores above 140 (Flynn, 35). For American whites, data based on derivatives of the Binet test have shown an increase in IQ of 25 points from 1918 to 1995 (Flynn, 37). Flynn's work has now achieved the status of a shorthand title, the Flynn Effect, and the American Psychological Association recently devoted a book, The Rising Curve, to scientific papers discussing and debating it. Many of the issues raised are directly relevant to this book. For example, IQ and various achievement test scores of both black and Hispanic students did indeed have lower means for decades, but since 1970 they have been increasing faster than have test scores for whites (Grissmer et al. 1998) and are converging with white scores (Hauser; Ceci, Rosenblum, and Kumpf). The bell curve is also changing shape; there is less of a difference currently between the very highest and lowest 20% for the verbal portion of tests given to high school juniors (Ceci, Rosenblum, and Kumpf). The crucial point of the Flynn Effect is that whatever IQ tests are measuring, it is influenced by forces other than genetics, and such tests are not a valid support for the old eugenics argument of a master race.

Gardner's Multiple Intelligences

In contrast to IQ, the emerging paradigm in intelligence studies seems to be multiple intelligences, as first and perhaps best proposed by Howard Gardner (1983). Gardner's work, and the many ideas that have developed from it, are beyond the main focus of this book, but Gardner's most important proposal is that there are several forms of human intelligence, and these are probably more or less genetically independent of each other. That is, someone who inherits natural abilities in one type of intelligence may or may not be gifted in other areas; a logical implication is that typically an individual would be born with a mixture of strengths, weaknesses, and average abilities in different areas.

Gardner's original proposal was for at least seven intelligences: *logical-mathematical; linguistic,* especially skill in one's native tongue, for the ability to learn second languages might be yet a different type of linguistic intelligence; *spatial,* conceptualizing in three dimensions, abilities an architect, quarterback, or general would use; *musical,* in which various researchers have noted that giftedness in logical-mathematical thought is often found with musical ability, but not always vice versa; *kinesthetic,* involving directed control of the whole body, such as an accomplished dancer uses; *interpersonal,* which a good salesperson uses; *intrapersonal,* which is the ability to understand and assess one's self.

Geometry as a Metaphor for Intelligence

The concept of multiple intelligences may also reflect increasing familiarity among scientists with statistical ideas not based on a simple, linear number line. The development of computers assisted in popularizing techniques to simultaneously make comparisons based on numerous variables. Comparisons of three variables can still be graphed on three-dimensional axes. Beyond three dimensions, comparisons can no longer be visualized by the human mind, but there are techniques in which different groups are compared based on 100 or even more variables, such as in the genetic comparisons of human populations done by Cavalli-Sforza et al. Such analysis of n-dimensional spaces began in number-crunching military intelligence approaches but found its way into biology through uses in taxonomy or ecology. This idea of visualizing human abilities or genetic variability as a geometric figure of multiplied n-dimensions would have been very difficult for the Victorian-era scientists who were baffled by Mendel's 2 x 2 tables.

Comparison of cultures by estimates of different types of intelligence reveals that each society has different standards of achievement, and who is a high achiever will thus vary in part on what particular type of intelligence is most valued in that setting and how that intelligence is trained to be used. Ogbu of the University of California—Berkeley has done interesting work in studying these relationships. For example, urban children of European ancestry in Australia tend to do well on logical-mathematical tests but poorly on spatial intelligence tests, whereas these results are reversed for Australian aborigine children in rural areas; this reflects underlying priorities in what children are taught in the two cultures (Ogbu). Within the framework of intelligence being manifold and multidimensional, there is debate whether there are only seven types of intelligence, or perhaps several more, but no disagreement that ranking humans by a single number line has been nonsense.

GENETIC REDUCTIONISM

In the nineteenth century, the problem was that Mendel was not understood; in the twentieth century, his work was understood but has sometimes been misapplied. There is no more debate regarding particulate inheritance, but sometimes particles have been invented to fit a social need. Two examples illustrate the danger of DNA sequences replacing craniometry and IQ tests as the potential reductionist fallacy of the next century.

The So-Called Criminal Gene

In the 1960s, the trait double Y was discovered: men with two Y chromosomes instead of one. The Y chromosome controls the male sex hormone testosterone and determines development as a boy baby rather than a girl baby. With two Ys, these men receive a double dose of testosterone and tend to be larger and more muscular than the average male. It was later discovered that a number of prominent and particularly brutal criminals were YY. At one point in the 1970s, there was a serious proposal in the Boston area to identify all YYs at birth, for lifetime surveillance (Hubbard and Wald, 106).

More careful follow-up revealed that only a minority of YY men are criminals, and of course crimes are committed by men and women of all kinds of genetic background. In addition, definitions of aggression and crime vary greatly among societies and over time. Presumably the double Ys were feared for violent muggings or something similar, not for quietly embezzling millions from a bank. Duster and Hubbard and Wald give good but brief reviews (Duster 1990, 30–32, 41; Hubbard and Wald, 104–6). The idea of the criminal gene illustrates three important errors: that categories of "criminal" and "noncriminal" are distinct and fixed throughout life, that they are heavily biological in origin, and that a single genetic difference can account for the categories.

Homosexuality: A Behavior or an Identity?

Until the twentieth century, the prevailing view in the English-speaking world was that sex between men and men or women and women was sinful behavior in the eyes of God. It was, however, still a behavior. In the twentieth century behavior became being. That is, "homosexual" describes what an individual is, not what he or she does. One would expect motivations in sexual behavior, like intelligence, criminality, or any other aspect of human personality, to be complex, multifaceted, and sometimes ambiguous.

Simon LaVey of the Salk Institute in San Diego studied volumes of various cellular regions of the hypothalamus region of the brain in nineteen homosexual men who had died of AIDS; sixteen "presumed heterosexual" men, six of whom died of AIDS; and six "presumed heterosexual" women. The average volume of one of the four cell groupings in the hypothalamus region that he followed was smaller in this sample of homosexual men and heterosexual women than it was in heterosexual men; however, the range of sizes in each sample was similar. The heterosexual men who died of AIDS on average also had smaller volumes. LaVey concluded that this volumetric difference was associated with sexual orientation and "suggests that sexual orientation has a biological substrate" (LaVey). LaVey, who is gay, felt he had a mission to demonstrate a biological basis for homosexual behavior. In an interview with *Newsweek,* for example, he was quoted as saying: "I felt if I didn't find any [difference in the hypothalamuses] I would give up a scientific career altogether" (Gelman et al. 1992). Besides the fact that LaVey is not neutral in his research goals, criticisms of his paper have included the small sample size, the use of nominal categories for a complex of behaviors and attitudes, and the general approach of using brain statistics to group humans, as Broca did in the nineteenth century to prove the inferiority of women or non-Europeans.

In 1993 I had the opportunity to hear Troy Duster speak on genetic reductionism at a conference on science and moral values. Addressing the topic of his book, *Backdoor to Eugenics,* in the second half of his talk he used LaVey's paper as a case study of the readiness of society to accept a reductionist genetic argument. Even within LaVey's paper, although he is writing from a position of advocacy, there is no suggestion of single gene control of gayness, only a proposed association with an anatomical trait. Duster followed coverage of LaVey's paper in the popular press and documented how, within a short time, the results had mutated into discovery of a "gay gene"; within days, the quotation marks were dropped, and within a few weeks, pundits in newspapers as prestigious as the *New York Times* were debating the significance of the gay gene, as though it were an established fact.

Duster, who is African American, devoted a portion of the first half of his talk to use of genetic language historically in the oppression of blacks. His concern in reviewing the reception to LaVey was to show that there still exists a belief that single genes destine a person to be one thing or another.

His book, like Gould's, is an excellent discussion of past abuses but goes further to discuss present problems, such as widespread use of abortion in many countries to select children, as well as how these precedents might be extended in future misuse of genetic data through reductionist genetic hypotheses. As an example of what has occurred already, a study in Bombay in the 1980s revealed that of 8,000 abortions, 7,997 were of female babies (Duster 1993, 33). Technically, compulsory sterilization by government authorities for genetic reasons is still fully legal in the United States (Duster 1993, 30), although it is not practiced. Short of sterilization, no one knows how far the authority of health insurance providers extends in demanding genetic screening, or how far insurance providers could go in denying coverage for "defective" alleles, particularly newly proposed genetic traits such as addiction.

Science is a process for getting relative answers about what can be measured. It serves us well, but science cannot speak to what we should do or to why we exist. In this chapter we have seen how many scientists and other intellectual opinion leaders of the past two centuries echoed the morality of their culture in bolstering racism rather than being as objective as they were assumed to be. In the next chapters we will examine whether the Bible addresses the concept of race and the purpose of humanity.

CHAPTER 9

■

A Christian Perspective on Race: Personal Reflections

W E HAVE NOW REVIEWED WHAT I HOPE IS A TRUSTWORTHY sample of the historical and scientific data that illuminate the idea of race as a false and shoddy myth. None of us is or shall ever be the evolutionary "superman" envisioned by Haeckel. Having established that the category of race does *not* provide the basis for our human identity, do we have a positive insight to build upon or only the negative command to reject race and racism? To address these questions, I give you here my personal perspective, as a Christian and as a geneticist, with a life experience flavored by living in several diverse places.

THE BASIS OF HUMAN IDENTITY

The Bible is not a book about science. Neither is it in conflict with science. However, it *is* in conflict with what has been called scientism, the attempt to extend the scientific method to a worldview or philosophy that refuses to consider the existence of a spiritual world. In contrast, Galileo saw no conflict between the Bible and science when he said, "The Bible tells us how to go to heaven, not how the heavens go." What then can we learn at the intersection of the Bible and biology about the purpose for our lives?

While science is a powerful key to many kinds of knowledge, it is limited to whatever can be measured. All people, even those who most strongly believe that only the material world exists, have to make moral decisions for which there is no physical measurement. People in all places and times know innately that there is a difference between good and evil, even when they may struggle with defining these.

The Bible attributes this knowledge of a moral standard to God's grace in our lives (Romans 2:15). The secular foundation of much of our present education and public policy, however, has created a type of insoluble problem for itself as it ignores the existence of God's moral law. We want people to treat each other decently, yet if human existence is nothing but a fluke in the universe, if all our actions are only vehicles ultimately for reproducing our DNA—one more generation driven by the "selfish gene," as biologist Richard Dawkins has put it—what real reason is there for decent behavior?

What Does It Mean to Be Human?

In its opening pages, the Bible attributes the creation, including living creatures, to God's work. Humanity—male and female—is said to bear "the image of God" (Genesis 1:27). Later, the Bible records what theologians refer to as the Fall (Genesis 3): the rejection of God's authority and a severing of a right relationship between humanity and God and among individuals. All of this is information that cannot be confirmed by science. Yet an appreciation of the image of God and the fall of humanity from grace gives us the ability to live in a world of people in a way that the study of only that which is measurable never can.

On the one hand, this means that because all humans are sinners and their cultures also have the potential to be evil, we stand in need of a Savior to restore us to relationship with God. On the other hand, it means that there are no individuals or people groups anywhere whose existence and culture lack value, because every human being is a bearer of the image of God. The hand of God molded the system of genetic diversity (Psalm 139:13–16), including those characteristics we have falsely distinguished as racial traits. Anyone who disparages the architecture disparages the Architect.

Personal Identity

Identity, an accurate and appropriate understanding of oneself, is often a casualty of racism and bigotry. At the American Antislavery Society in 1837, an African American delegate confessed to the convention that "many among us have tacitly consented to admit that we were an inferior race" (Goodman, 256). Contemporary African American Christians such as Tony Evans and Jefferson Edwards stress the same point, recognizing the impact that the myth of an inferior race has had throughout our culture, and especially among blacks (e.g., Edwards, 17–19; Evans, 1–20). For example, Edwards describes the mental dilemma of African American students who may assume that they are the only ones who are struggling in a course, when in reality the entire class is having difficulty. Because of the myth of the inferior race, it is all too easy for such students to accept an identity of being "at risk," to begin to believe that there is some sort of genetic block that inhibits learning.

As a teacher, I observe that many, perhaps even most college students of all backgrounds struggle with their identity, with knowing their purpose and calling in life. Part of the ministry of Jesus was to free the oppressed (Luke 4:18), and surely an aspect of that calling is restoring an accurate and healthy self-identity to anyone who feels inferior. To know who we are, we need God's assessment of us. We need to know God's purpose for our existence, both generally and personally; otherwise we will be left to assess our identity only by the mirror of the reactions of the people in our society.

REVELATIONS OF GOD

The Bible speaks of several means through which God has revealed himself. The entire creation, for example, is a type of nonverbal revelation of the Creator (e.g., Psalm 19:1–3; Romans 1:20). The Bible claims to be the verbal revelation of that otherwise unknowable Creator (e.g., Psalm 19:7–9; 2 Timothy 3:15–16, and many other passages). Thus, God has revealed understanding about himself. Consider the mystery of this concept. The Creator of a universe unimaginably huge and old and complex is presented as communicating directly to humans in their languages, within their cultures. Jesus the Messiah, the ultimate mystery of revelation, is the invisible made visible. God chose to communicate with humans by allowing the infinite Son to take on a finite human body and to bring the gospel message to a world in need of salvation. Jesus himself embodied the message of God's love for all.

The Bible on Race

Although a complete study of this question would require a book in and of itself, allow me to highlight several points about what the Bible says on the topic of race. First, the Bible carries a message in what is not said: There is a striking lack of physical description throughout the Scriptures, such description being almost totally absent in the New Testament. This "omission" is consistent with God's word to Samuel not to look at outward appearance, but at the heart (1 Samuel 16:7).

Race in the Old Testament Regardless of whether the first chapters of Genesis are interpreted as expressing human beginnings literally or poetically, only one human race is presented. This perspective holds true throughout the Bible (see 1 Corinthians 15:22). Even the two classic proof-texts of racists—Cain's mark in Genesis 4:1–17 and the curse of Ham in Genesis 9:20–27—do not support the concept of distinctive "races" when examined. Cain is interpreted by New Testament writers as a dangerous metaphor for how jealousy over God's blessing can lead to murderous behavior (1 John 3:11–12; Jude 11). The warning is that the potential to be a Cain is in each of us. There is no clue in the Bible what the "mark" on Cain might have been, nor any indication that it was something his descendents would inherit. Moreover, the purpose of the mark was so that no other person would take vengeance on Cain (Genesis 4:15), not to identify him as fit for oppression as has been argued by racist apologists in the past.

Similarly, Noah's curse on Ham (whom Scripture says was the father of many North African nations) makes no mention of any physical manifestation. In fact, the curse is placed on Canaan alone of Ham's four sons-not on Ham himself or on the sons whose descendents populated Africa. And beyond these shaky foundations for racial oppression that have been built on this text, in the context of Israel's history, the curse seems to be fulfilled when the Jews, descendents of Shem, took possession of the land of Canaan. The Bible never refers to the curse again, and Judah, the tribe of both David and Jesus, even originated from the union of Jewish and Canaanite DNA (see Genesis 38).

When one studies the pedigrees of the people of Israel, it is clear, from numerous cases, that ethnic boundaries were rarely a barrier to marriage, neither did they prohibit people from different nations from making a covenant with the God of Abraham. (See Genesis 38:2,6; 41:45; Exodus 2:16,21; Numbers 12:1–2; Joshua 2:11; 2 Samuel 15:21; Jeremiah 38:7–13, among many other biblical texts that illustrate this point.)

Race in the New Testament And what of the New Testament? What did Jesus and his followers have to say about race—or about how God relates to people of different ethnic heritage? Jesus himself antagonized his fellow Jews as he stressed that God's covenant is not based on ethnic heritage (Luke 4:26–30; John 4:22–24). Although breaking down traditional barriers between nationalities sometimes required miraculous acts of God, slowly the

Jewish followers of Jesus learned to welcome Samaritans (Acts 8:4–6), Ethiopians (Acts 8:26–29), Italians (Acts 10:1,47), Greeks (Acts 11:20), and eventually anyone who came to Christ as Lord (Acts 15).

Scripture's final word on national and ethnic identity occurs in Revelation, which describes the vision John saw before the throne of God of "a great multitude that no one could count" (Revelation 7:9). That multitude included every *ethnos*, a Greek word translated as "nation," and every laos, the root of our English "laity" which is often translated as "people," and every language. Completely absent in this apocalyptic and prophetic text is a description suggesting "races" as Western and Islamic worlds have conceived.

Each Christian Called to Be a Revelation

Another form of revelation that is sometimes overlooked is that of individual Christian lives. In 2 Corinthians 3:3 Paul refers to Christian believers as "letters from Christ." This does not mean each believer makes up religious ideas as he or she goes along; rather, as we follow Jesus Christ, and as his Spirit works through us, we ourselves become not only a messenger but a message as well. We become the Word of God lived out, no longer just abstract propositions but choices of will in lives that involve sacrifice and joy.

Bryant Myers describes it this way: Christians are called to live "eloquent lives" (Myers, 18). This also is a mystery, but it's real! Furthermore, God is interested in writing his message in all contexts. Whatever your personal, family, and ethnic background is, if you belong to Jesus, your life is intended to be a letter from God, and it cannot be duplicated by anyone else. We communicate what we are, not just through abstract ideas, but with our lives, just as Jesus' life, in addition to his words, was a message. Each life—your life, my life—is potentially a letter with a unique context in which Christ writes his gospel.

We see this illustrated in each of the unusual and unique people God used throughout scriptural history. Have you ever noticed, for example, how many people in the Bible whom God used in a special way had crossed cultural frontiers in some way? Sometimes it even happened because of domination or oppression. They had complex personal histories. For example, Daniel and Esther lived outside of Israel because of the conquering of Israel by a foreign power, and God used them to profoundly affect the nations in which they were ethnic outsiders. The multicultural childhoods of Moses and Paul prepared them to communicate God's words to audiences from

Pharaoh or Caesar to slaves, prisoners, and prison guards. Joseph, who rose to great authority in Egypt, saved both his extended family and the Egyptians. Joseph became a fully bicultural and bilingual man through it, prepared for the fulfillment of his dream in a way he never imagined.

Likewise, every experience in a person's life can affect that person positively or negatively. Paul Tournier, a Swiss Christian and medical doctor, has written extensively on the relationships among physical, mental, and spiritual health. In *The Violence Within* he documents and develops the theme of how often leadership arises out of "abnormal or frustrating family circumstances" (Tournier, 138–142). Enormous numbers of world leaders were orphans or born out of wedlock or separated from parents by traumatic circumstances. This discussion takes place within the context of the danger of abusing authority once one has been entrusted with it, but the point still stands. What destroys one person, can cause another to develop depth of character-or depth of hatred and bitterness-that draws others to follow their vision.

As John Perkins struggled with physical and spiritual recovery after he was beaten by Mississippi troopers, he reached a similar conclusion: "What doesn't destroy me, makes me stronger" (Perkins 1976, 205). God's calling for us is that love would overpower hate. This is possible only when the love of Christ within us makes us more than conquerors (Romans 8; Perkins 1976, 205).

The message of the parable of the good Samaritan (Luke 10:25–37) is that God-ordained and God-pleasing mercy crosses all ethnic barriers. A Christian who has faith in God's providence may ultimately be able to say, as Joseph said to his brothers who sold him into slavery, "You intended to harm me, but God intended it for good to accomplish what is now being done, the saving of many lives" (Genesis 50:20). God desires to write a unique message of reconciliation if Christians in the United States and elsewhere can put away the concept and sin of race. Perhaps David Walker's vision in the early 1800s— that God would use black Christians to convert whites to the color blindness of the gospel—shall yet be fulfilled. Who knows what God may accomplish through us if we can work together for Christ's kingdom?

RECONCILIATION AND PEACEMAKING

When I was a graduate student at the University of Minnesota in St. Paul, I became acquainted with an anthropologist and missions professor from Bethel (Baptist) Seminary named Herb Klem and later attended his course in cross-cultural communications. Herb had recently moved to Minnesota after twelve years of Christian ministry and seminary teaching in a predominantly Yoruba region of West Africa.. The Yoruba are a large ethnic group, particularly prominent in the history and culture of Nigeria, and many Yoruba were among the slaves brought to the Americas. Yoruba culture stresses corporate identity: membership in a family line, in a clan, in a nation, and so on. (Tony Evans has included a fascinating section in *Let's Get to Know Each Other* about the Yoruba worldview and religion, which helped shape African American Christianity [Evans, 490–59].)

In his class, Herb often stressed the challenge and the value of the perspective that each culture in the world brings to the Bible. One day a student suddenly asked him how his own perspective had changed from his years of immersion in Yoruba thought and culture. Herb shared that he had gradually realized that one way that he approached many Bible passages as a North American was to unconsciously think of relationship with God primarily on an individual level, whereas the Yoruba Christians would see God at work across the generations in a family or within a people or political country.

The Yoruba perspective is very biblical. For example, God did not call only Abraham; God was also at work in the lives of his sons and grandsons and great-grandsons, and on and on. And so it must be with you and me. When we come to know Christ as our Savior, we are called by God not only as individuals but as intercessors for the corporate realities to which we belong-to our own extended families, our neighborhoods, our people, our countries, our world. This is an important part of what the Bible means when it refers to all believers as priests (1 Peter 2:5,9).

Desire for Reconciliation among Peoples

In spite of all the atrocities and racism of the past five centuries, there remains a deep desire for reconciliation in the hearts of many people of the Americas. Conrad Phillip Kottak, author of a widely used undergraduate text on anthropology, sees both the holiday of Thanksgiving in the United States and television shows such as *Star Trek* and *Star Trek: Next Generation* as reflecting an American dream of different kinds of people living together in peace and surviving, perhaps even thriving, by drawing on each others' strengths (Kottak, 387–90). That is, of all the events that occurred in the founding of the thirteen colonies prior to the American Revolution, we remember and reenact a day of peace between the Pilgrims and the Native Americans, when God was thanked and the Native Americans were also thanked, and all sat to eat together. I do not know how Kottak, apparently a secular anthropologist, ultimately views this dream, but as a Christian I believe it is an echo of the need God placed in us for human friendship.

As Kottak notes, each of the *Star Trek* series is a dream of a future in which different peoples, this time even from different stars, succeed in living together and learning to reconcile their animosities. We can see this longing in other American movies and television shows as well.

One good example of this is the 1986 movie *Places in the Heart*, about a widow in a small Texas cotton town and the people around her. The powerful ending places all the protagonists of the film together, receiving Communion in a Baptist church. The force of this final scene builds as the camera pans from person to person while the Communion plate is passed and each person pronounces the blessing of the "peace of Christ" to the next as they take the bread and wine. There are several people we don't know; then we suddenly see an estranged couple now reunited, then a righteous black man driven from town by the Ku Klux Klan but now present with the white family whose farm he had saved, then the widow, then her late husband, who is now alive. Finally, her resurrected husband passes the Communion plate to the black man next to him, the man who had shot him accidentally and subsequently had been killed by a white mob, and he blesses him with the peace of Christ.

Martin Luther King Jr. put into words this longing for reconciliation in his well-loved speech given in 1963 at the march on Washington:

> I have a dream that one day this nation will rise up and live out the true meaning of its creed: "We hold these truths to be self-evident that all men are created equal."
>
> I have a dream that one day on the red hills of Georgia the sons of former slaves and the sons of former slaveowners will be able to sit down together at the table of brotherhood. . . .
>
> I have a dream that one day down in Alabama with its vicious racists, with its governor having his lips dripping with the words of interposition and nullification—one day right there in Alabama, little black boys and black girls will be able to join hands with little white boys and white girls as sisters and brothers.

I have a dream today.

I have a dream that one day every valley shall be exalted, every hill and mountain shall be made low, the rough places will be made plain and the crooked places will be made straight, and the glory of the Lord shall be revealed, and all flesh shall see it together. . . .

I believe the same longing for peace and reconciliation exists in Latin America within the concept of *La Raza*: that the ancient hostilities of the Spanish conquistador, the vanquished Native American, and the exiled African slave would be healed in the blended blood of their children, "the (new) race."

Corporate Reconciliation

John Dawson of Youth With A Mission has helped found a ministry that works to implement corporate reconciliation. He has outlined four steps toward corporate reconciliation: *confession,* involving truthfulness about who was wronged and how; *repentance,* which must involve action and change of behavior; *reconciliation,* expressing and receiving forgiveness and pursuing fellowship with former enemies; *restitution,* when possible, and seeking to do justice in any way that we have power to act or influence.

Dawson presents several case studies of corporate reconciliation. In the Sand Creek, Colorado, massacre of 1864, the U.S. Army, led by a former Methodist pastor, rode into a village of unarmed Arapaho and Cheyenne who were trusting in a federal treaty. Many Native Americans were shot as they attempted to demonstrate their peaceful intent by gathering around the American flag that was flying at the center of their village. The soldiers massacred 133 unarmed people, most of them women and children, and then mutilated the bodies, including cutting open pregnant women. Indian body parts were later displayed as trophies by the soldiers in various Colorado towns. Colonel John Chivington, the former pastor, had fought against slavery during the Civil War but issued orders in this case to "kill Cheyennes whenever and wherever found." The nearest town to the massacre site is today named Chivington after him (Dawson, 137–54).

Dawson believes this event has long been one of the roots of a spiritual stronghold of evil in the U.S. West, an event all Native Americans are familiar with, even when it is neglected by the rest of the culture. He believes that (consistent with Scripture), there is a curse on the land for violating covenants (Isaiah 24:5–6) and for shedding innocent blood (Numbers

35:33). In his book, Dawson describes at length how meetings of sustained confession and repentance and steps toward reconciliation were organized, and some of the effects of these. It was not flippantly or casually done, and people representing the parties involved, both Native American and white, and career U.S. Army officers, were involved. The meetings had profound effects on a number of lives (Dawson, 154–58).

In another case, Dawson describes how three innocent black men were lynched by a mob of thousands in Springfield, Missouri, in 1906, and how twenty-five churches, black and white, joined together in 1992 to ask God's forgiveness, and, on the part of the historically white churches, the forgiveness of black Christians (Dawson, 212–14). Wherever he is invited to speak, Dawson probes American Christians concerning what went on in their area during the days of slavery and segregation and whether steps toward repentance and reconciliation have ever been taken by black and white Christians. Dawson sees this as the great unfinished business of the church in the United States before it can experience an effective ministry in our society as we find it (Dawson, 214–19).

The late Spencer Perkins and Chris Rice, in their book, share the story of Kay Muller, from Evanston, Illinois, a suburb immediately to the north of Chicago (113–15). She discovered that in the 1800s her church, First Baptist of Evanston, had relegated black members to the balcony. This had led to black members forming their own church, Second Baptist, in 1873, and ever since the Baptists in Evanston had remained segregated. She initiated a process that led to a formal and unanimous confession of the sin of racism by members of First Baptist to members of Second Baptist, and the first joint worship service in 120 years. She and her church accepted the example of Nehemiah's confessing the sins of earlier generations of the Israelites as his own (Nehemiah 1:4–1).

TO BE CHRISTIAN IS TO BE A PEACEMAKER

Those who belong to Jesus Christ have been given the ministry of reconciliation (2 Corinthians 5:18–19). This means many things, but it does not mean the pretense of attempting to reconcile by politely removing the subject of the history of racism from the dinner table. All Christians are priests (2 Peter 2:5), able to intercede for their people to God. The most effective form of this prayer, Jesus tells us, will be that which receives no public recognition

(Matthew 6:6), but of course it does not end there. A healthy example of this is the speech of Mike Huckabee, governor of Arkansas, at the fortieth anniversary of the desegregation of Central High School in Little Rock, speaking to the white violence that accompanied those events in 1957:

> Essentially, it's not just a skin problem, it's a sin problem. Because we in Arkansas have wandered around in ambiguity, all kinds of explanations and justifications, and I think today we come to say once and for all that what happened here 40 years ago was simply wrong. It was evil. And we renounce it. (quoted in Enda)

Cardinal Anthony Bevilacqua: A Pastoral Letter

In Philadelphia, following some ugly racial brawls that involved people from an ethnic social club, the Roman Catholic cardinal, Anthony Bevilacqua, issued a pastoral letter. In it he stressed that the Bible shows us that racism separates us not only from others but also from God: "Whoever does not love does not know God" (1 John 4:8). He described the irony of the American Catholic community, often predominantly immigrant and suffering discrimination itself, acquiring the racist worldview inherited from the days of slavery. Although political and economic questions are clearly implied, "since racism is fundamentally a moral evil against the nature of the human person, its elimination requires ultimately a moral solution" (Bevilacqua, 6).

He closes the pastoral letter with an analogy based on Peter's encounter with Jesus at the Sea of Galilee, after Peter had denied Christ three times (John 21). The essence of Peter's denial, says Bevilacqua, was accommodation to gain acceptance. American Christians, like Peter, have repeatedly denied Christ when we have been guilty of racism. Yet Jesus does not cast our lives away but still invites us to his side, forgives, and sends us forth to do his will. Christianity is an incarnational religion, for us as well as for our Lord, and our call is thus to live God's truth. Cardinal Bevilacqua requests all churches in his pastoral care to find "innovative and visible ways" to show that all people are welcome.

John Lewis: An African American Congressman

Another example of an individual striving to be a peacemaker is John Lewis, a five-term congressman from Georgia who was prominent throughout the civil rights movement. He tells the story of his life in *Walking with the Wind: A Memoir of the Movement,* which won the 1999 Robert F. Kennedy Book Award.

Lewis was born the third child of black sharecroppers in Pike County, Alabama. Many of the whites as well as the blacks were poor, with a small group of wealthy whites controlling the local economy. There was a long history of racial oppression: for example, two churches near where he grew up were burned in 1904, because "they were the houses of worship of Negroes" (according to the report in the local paper; Lewis and D'Orso, 21). Troy, the nearest town, erected a monument in honor of John Wilkes Booth, the assassin of Abraham Lincoln (Lewis and D'Orso, 47). Lewis grew up in a devoutly Christian home. He describes with deep affection the services in the little country churches and his calling to be a preacher, including sermons he used to give to the family chickens as a child (Lewis and D'Orso, 34–40). He was disillusioned, however, with many of the traditional black preachers, who lived better than their flocks did and who avoided addressing the pains of daily life as a black in the South (Lewis and D'Orso, 55), as well as the way Christians often treated each other with cruelty (Lewis and D'Orso, 60–61).

When he was fifteen, Lewis heard Martin Luther King Jr. on the radio for the first time, and this changed his life, cementing his desire to be a preacher who spoke to human needs (Lewis and D'Orso, 56, 61). He was later able to attend an all-black seminary in Nashville, Tennessee. Here he met a man named James Lawson, who was teaching a well thought-out Christian pacifism and social gospel (Lewis and D'Orso, 83–87). This included the concept of redemptive suffering, the power released when a just person chooses to suffer injustice and forgive the oppressor (Lewis and D'Orso, 86). Like King, Lawson stressed that the means and the end are inseparable and that even the hateful must be responded to with love, not just as a political movement but as a way of life.

Out of the context of a philosophy of Christian pacifism and service, Lewis became involved in a campaign to desegregate lunch counters in Nashville; in 1961 he became one of the early Freedom Riders protesting bus segregation in the South. For that, he was severely beaten in Montgomery, Alabama, as the police stood by (Lewis and D'Orso, 157–62). In each setting, the emphasis was on love and nonviolence, stressing the teachings of Christ, Gandhi, and King (Lewis and D'Orso, 105–6). He helped to organize and, from 1963 to

1966, was chair of the Student Nonviolent Coordinating Committee (SNCC), which spearheaded much of the voter registration among blacks in the South. He was present and was beaten at the 1965 "Bloody Sunday" attack by Alabama troopers on unarmed civil rights marchers.

As the 1960s progressed and the social scene in the United States became increasingly chaotic, the SNCC grew divided over whether to hold to nonviolence and whether to continue as a multiracial organization (Lewis and D'Orso, 248, 365). Lewis held and still holds to both principles, and this directly contributed to his ouster as chair and later to his leaving the SNCC (Lewis and D'Orso, 363–74). Later in his book, he shows how the same convictions became the basis for his opposition to Louis Farrakhan and Khalid Muhummad of the Nation of Islam: The latter, speaking at Kean College in New Jersey, praised Hitler for his killing of the Jews and called for genocide against whites in South Africa (Lewis and D'Orso, 471–72). Lewis describes this as following "my conscience not my complexion" (Lewis and D'Orso, 469), and, citing "an obligation to condemn speech that is racist, bigoted, anti-Semitic or hateful" (Lewis and D'Orso, 469), he declined to participate in the Million Man March because of Farrakhan's central role in it.

John Perkins: Called to Return to the Fire

A third example of a peacemaker, John Perkins, is of personal interest: my wife and I met while we were working in Mississippi for the ministry that John founded.

John Perkins tells his story in *Let Justice Roll Down*. Many of his ideas on Christian community development are discussed further in *With Justice for All*. One of his gifts has been to identify and train subsequent generations of leaders. Dolphus Weary, one of the men who succeeded him in leadership, has told his own story, rich in insights, in *I Ain't Comin' Back*. John's late son, Spencer Perkins, and his friend and associate Chris Rice wrote *More Than Equals: Racial Healing for the Sake of the Gospel*, a book that sets out the issues and implications for Christians who want to break down racism.

Perkins and most of the leaders he has discipled grew up in southern Mississippi, between Jackson and the Gulf Coast. Perkins barely knew his father, who visited only once or twice, and he was reared by a grandmother active in bootlegging. After his older brother was gunned down by a white man, with no justice served, he left for California vowing never to return. He married and became a successful southern California business-man. Through a children's Sunday school, Perkins became interested in the Bible, opened his life to Christ, and began to involve himself in ministries.

Eventually Perkins felt that God was calling him to return to Mississippi. He and his wife, Vera Mae, began Bible classes for children and teenagers, which were very successful. Because of the many community problems, step by step they found themselves adding programs related to physical and social needs. Eventually they became involved in voter registration and finally in an economic boycott in response to a gross violation of the law by local police. This made Perkins a marked man, and in February 1970 he was ambushed by a gang of police in Brandon, Mississippi, and was tortured and brutally beaten. His firsthand encounter with such demonic violence changed his ministry.

During his lengthy recovery, Perkins wrestled with whether the gospel of Christ was having any effect on shattering racism in Mississippi. He was led by God to understand that the white policemen were also victims of racism. They were mostly from poor backgrounds, and much of their self-esteem came only from being able to abuse yet poorer blacks. God gave Perkins a compassion for white racists, based on Jesus' forgiveness of those who crucified him. Perkins writes about how, as he lay recovering, he prayed one by one for each policeman whose face he could remember, seeking to obey the command to "overcome evil with good" (Romans 12:21). Spencer Perkins said the night of the beating changed not just the family's lives but also their Christianity: from that time on, they realized fully that the gospel must include reconciliation to others or it is not the true gospel (Perkins and Rice, 44).

John Perkins continues to live out his beliefs, and he and his associates continue to seek God's leading as they try creative new approaches. Ten years to the day after Perkins's beating, the governor of Mississippi honored him as "outstanding religious leader of the year."

The examples of these peacemakers show "the most excellent way" (1 Corinthians 12:31), one that each of us can follow. May we be inspired to work toward reconciliation in ways that use our unique gifts.

A LIFE OF CHRISTIAN RECONCILIATION

Jesus promised that those who would follow him would always be a minority in the world (Matthew 7:13–14); nonetheless, they would have an influence beyond their numbers, being salt to prevent the rot in the meat of society (Matthew 5:13) and a light in a dark room (Matthew 5:14–16). Among the many fruits of this teaching has been the role of the Christian man or woman who has challenged prevailing authority and appealed to the conscience of the nation on the basis of God's eternal standard of justice.

To be able to present such a challenge to society, we must face the facts of our history. Where they are the facts of our personal or family history in some way, we as Christians may have the opportunity to serve as priests in a special way, confessing the sins of our people as our own. We all need to guard against being smug about our own apparent freedom from racism. It is far too easy for all of us to see the speck in another's eye and miss the log in our own (Matthew 7:3). For William Lloyd Garrison in the 1800s, slavery was "strictly a national sin" (Goodman, 40). That is, he did not consider the Southern whites more deeply in guilt than the Northern whites; slavery was a sin that called for repentance by the whole country. Unfortunately, after Lincoln's assassination, some of the federal policies and practices that developed reflected a type of vengeance against the South as a defeated, evil enemy, rather than a national recognition of the sin of slavery. This ultimately resulted in bitterness rather than healing and has been seen as a contributing factor to the rise of terrorist organizations like the Ku Klux Klan.

I myself had to struggle with bitterness against the Southern Baptists after several small but ugly incidents. For example, while living in Mississippi, Chris, my future wife, and I were invited by a friendly Christian woman to her Southern Baptist church, which, she assured us, was open to "everyone," including Chris's roommate, who was an African American Christian woman from Pittsburgh. It was very close to the Fourth of July weekend in 1976, and the church had prepared a special Sunday evening program about religious liberty in celebration of the United States bicentennial. The three of us went and seemed to be received by everyone with real Christian hospitality, even being invited to a dessert social afterwards. We left feeling welcome to come again. Within less than a week, however, we learned that many people who were members but did not regularly attend were angry about our visit and were even lobbying for the pastor's resignation for allowing us in. We were sent a message through a third party: the church wanted no more visits from "blacks or Yankees."

Later, despite my bitterness over this and other incidents, we became members of a Southern Baptist church for several years while we were living in a particular locale. I look at this now as God's great sense of humor, but it was not an easy transition for me. I am ashamed today of those times when I was ungracious and bitter. This particular Southern Baptist church, however, was quite multiethnic and included interracial couples. I was forced to come to terms with the fact that God works among Southern whites as well as he works with sinful Swedes like me.

Prayer as a Tool to Fight Racism

Although some Christians will be called by God to serve honestly and justly in public office, most of us will not. But every Christian is commanded to pray. The Bible says that in prayer we have been given "divine power to demolish strongholds" (2 Corinthians 10:4). In that context, Paul speaks of demolishing strongholds in terms of demolishing "arguments and every pretension that sets itself up against the knowledge of God, and we take captive every thought to make it obedient to Christ" (v. 5). Strongholds can be long-established ways of thinking in a person or in a society. Racism is one such stronghold. John Perkins believes that for Americans at least, the command for Christians to "bear one another's burdens" must be recognized as including the effects of racism on blacks and whites (Perkins 1982, 109).

God's word to the people of Israel through Haggai was that they had returned from exile but had neglected repairing the temple of God because of their own busy agendas; as a result their enterprises had not prospered (Haggai 1:2–11). We, too, live with a shattered temple in our midst-the body of Christ mocked and crucified by five centuries of racism within the church. Although we are returning from a type of Babylonian exile that this deception has carried us to, the spiritual rebuilding has only begun. The spiritual task of Christians in this context must include joining with believers across ethnic lines to rebuild the temple of the Lord as it was intended to be.

Being Together

The book of Acts tells us that in a Spirit-filled church, believers enjoy eating together in their homes (Acts 2:46). Paul indicates that one of the first signs of not being true to living in Christ and Christ in us is ceasing to eat together and separating ethnically (Galatians 2:11–21). Reconciliation involves some type of active concern for the other. For this to occur, there have to be common meeting places and experiences, opportunities to reach out and to be vulnerable with someone we wouldn't ordinarily associate with. John Perkins notes how Jesus came to the Samaritan woman on her territory (John 4), and their conversation was started based on her felt needs (Perkins 1982, 52–53).

The character of the United States or any other country will ultimately not be decided by policy set in its capital but by the nature of the millions of relationships among its citizens. If those who know and love Jesus intentionally begin to seek to cross ethnic barriers to get to know others as individuals, that act will change both parties, and it will change the society's character, too.

Jefferson Edwards, in *Purging Racism from Christianity*, presents a good test: as a Christian, are you or would you be willing to learn regularly from a Christian leader of another ethnic background (Edwards, 29)? If not, why not? For the Student Nonviolent Coordinating Committee (SNCC) at the height of the civil rights movement, this became a critical issue. Well-meaning white college students would begin to dominate groups previously headed by less formally educated Southern blacks; sometimes they were explicit in expressing their motivation: atonement for their own guilt (Lewis and D'Orso, 243–46). This led to a reaction toward black separation that, among other things, ousted John Lewis as chair and removed white staff members (Lewis and D'Orso, 367).

During the years he headed Voice of Calvary Ministries in Mendenhall, Mississippi, John Perkins observed similar problems among some white evangelical volunteers. These specifically included problems with truly trusting black leadership or coming to a black community to relieve one's own guilt, without focusing on ministering to the needs of others (Perkins 1982, 84). Spencer Perkins and Chris Rice discuss frankly the emotionally intense struggles over balancing roles of blacks and whites within their church in Jackson, Mississippi (Perkins and Rice, 46–56, 131–42).

Perkins and Rice attributed their eventual working through of the differences to the recognition that reconciliation was a spiritual issue (Perkins and Rice, 142). For Rice, a white American, this included understanding that racial reconciliation was necessary not just to "do good" but because he needed it to be spiritually whole (Perkins and Rice, 136). The foundation for reconciliation cannot be merely removing racism or paternalism but building real trust (Perkins and Rice, 185). Besides the touchstone of willingness to submit to a leader of a different ethnic background, they ask other questions about level of trust, such as whether the race of a baby-sitter matters, or whether there is someone of a different background with whom one would pray regularly (Perkins and Rice, 75–76). All of these issues find parallels among the early Christians in the book of Acts and in the letter to the Galatians. After several church councils, Gentile Christians were finally seen as equals with Jewish Christians before God, but it was another step before they were truly friends and peers. To live as New Testament Christians, we too need to take that next step from doctrinal understanding to practical living.

EPILOGUE

———■———

When we've been there ten thousand years,
Bright shining as the sun,
We've no less days to sing God's praise,
Than when we've first begun.

O N OCTOBER 4, 1997, I AND MORE THAN A MILLION OTHERS attended the PromiseKeepers "Sacred Assembly—Stand in the Gap" in Washington, D.C.

I rode to and from Philadelphia on a chartered bus next to a Mexican American from Colorado. With some friends, I was squeezed into a standing-room-only space within sight of the stage. I was jammed between white Christians from Massachusetts and Florida, black Christians from Nebraska (Malcolm X's home state), and a vibrant group of Puerto Rican Christians. The assembly began with the sounding of a shofar and prayers by a group of Messianic Jews, consistent with God's promise to Abraham that through him, all the nations would be blessed. This opening prayer was coupled with one by an Iroquois pastor, in the full formal regalia of his people—and this was profoundly appropriate, for the political model of the Iroquois League may have contributed to the U.S. Constitution (Weatherford, 133–50). The worship, and what worship it was, with more than a million men singing, was initiated by Joe Garlington, a black pastor from Pittsburgh.

A significant portion of the time was set aside for confession of sins of racism and bigotry in the United States. More than a million men, many of them fasting for the assembly, prostrated themselves before God in the

Washington Mall to seek God's forgiveness personally and nationally for these evils. Some of the corporate prayers were led by people from many ethnic origins, each asking God's forgiveness for the sins of *their* people and asking for God's grace; white, black, Hispanic, Asian, Native American, and Jewish Christian leaders all led prayers. Although there were a number of women present, it seemed appropriate that since men had mostly created these problems, it was men who were repenting before God. No one individual dominated the proceedings; the speakers, worship leaders, and prayer leaders were diverse, and almost none spoke at length or led worship or prayers more than once or twice. The crowd was often directed to break into small groups to pray for one another concerning different issues. At one point, I was in an extended time of prayer with two black brothers from Omaha, Nebraska, for the evangelism of the world. The assembly was real and it was profound, and I know of no precedent for any spiritual event like this in the history of the Americas. May God grant us the grace to so continue to carry out the words of Christ, to seek the kingdom of God, and leave race behind us in history.

A FINAL WORD

In adding yet one more book to the many already written on the issue of race and ethnicity, I have often thought of the words of Ecclesiastes, "Of making of many books, there is no end" (Ecclesiastes 12:12). However, although that quote is well known, its context is not:

> *Now all has been heard;*
>> *here is the conclusion of the matter:*
> *Fear God and keep his commandments,*
>> *for this is the whole duty of man.*
> *For God will bring every deed into judgment,*
>> *including every hidden thing,*
>> *whether it is good or evil. (Ecclesiastes 12:13–14)*

The prophet Micah tells us more about the commandments of God:

> *He has showed you, O man, what is good,*
>> *And what does the LORD require of you?*
> *To act justly, and to love mercy*
>> *and to walk humbly with your God. (Micah 6:8)*

If this book has moved you toward thinking and living in that way, it has accomplished its purpose.

REFERENCES

Abanes, R. 1996. *Rebellion, racism and religion: American militias.* Downers Grove, Ill.: InterVarsity Press.

Allen, T. W. 1994. *The invention of the white race.* Vol. 1: *Racial oppression and social control.* London: Verso.

American Anthropological Association. 1998. AAA statement on race. *Anthropology Newsletter,* September, 3.

Appleton, J., et al., eds. 1978. *The Arabs: People and power.* New York: Encyclopaedia Britannica/Bantam Books.

Aristotle. 1946. *Politics.* Translated by E. Baker. Oxford: Oxford University Press.

Armour, J. A. L., et al. 1996. Minisatellite diversity supports a recent African origin for modern humans. *Nature Genetics* 13:154–60.

Augustine. *The city of God.* Book 16, chapter 8. Translated by J. H., George Eld., London.

Barnabas, S., R. V. Apte, and C. G. Suresh. 1996. Ancestry and interrelationships of the Indians and their relationship with other world populations: A study based on mitochondrial DNA polymorphisms. *Annals of Human Genetics* 60:409–22.

Barton, H. A., ed. 1975. *Letters from the promised land: Swedes in America, 1840–1914.* Minneapolis: University of Minnesota Press.

Beals, I. A. 1997. *Our racist legacy: Will the church resolve the conflict?* Notre Dame, Ind.: Cross Cultural Publications.

Bennett, L., Jr. 1969. *Before the Mayflower: A history of black America.* Chicago: Johnson Publishing.

Berry, W. 1989. *The hidden wound.* New York: North Point Press.

Bevilacqua, A. 1998. Healing racism through faith and truth. Pastoral letter, Archdiocese of Philadelphia, 6 January. Available on the Internet at http://archdiocese-phl.org

Birgander, R., et al. 1996. The codon 31 polymorphism of the p53–inducible gene p21 shows distinct differences between major ethnic groups. *Hum. Hered.* 46:148–54.

Blocher, H. 1979/1984. *In the beginning*. Translated by D. G. Preston. Downers Grove, Ill.: InterVarsity Press.

Blockson, C. L. 1987. *The underground railroad: Dramatic firsthand accounts of daring escapes to freedom*. New York: Berkeley.

Bortolini, M. C., et al. 1992. Genetic studies in three South American Black populations. *Gene Geography* 6:1–16.

Bouchard, T.J., Jr., et al. 1990. Sources of human psychological differences: The Minnesota study of twins reared apart. *Science* 250:223–50.

———. 1994. Genes, environment and personality. *Science* 264:1700–1701.

Burke, J. 1985. *The day the universe changed*. Boston: Little, Brown.

Cavalli-Sforza, L. L. 1991. Genes, people and languages. *Scientific American*, November, 104–10.

Cavalli-Sforza, L. L., P. Menozzi, and A. Piazza. 1994/1996 abridged version. *The history and geography of human genes*. Princeton, N.J.: Princeton University Press.

Ceci, S. J., T. B. Rosenblum, and M. Kumpf. 1998. The shrinking gap between high- and low-scoring groups: current trends and possible causes. In U. Neisser, ed., *The rising curve*, 287–302. Washington, D.C.: American Psychological Association.

Chakraborty, R., et al. 1992. Caucasian genes in American Blacks: New data. *Am. J. Hum. Genet.* 50:145–55

Christenson, L. 1975. Pentecostalism's forgotten forerunner. In V. Synan, ed., *Aspects of Pentecostal-charismatic origins*, 15–38. Plainfield, New Jersey: Logos International.

Coupland, R. 1933/1964. *The British anti-slavery movement*. New York: Barnes and Noble. Foreword to the 1964 edition is by J. D. Fage.

Cummings, M. R. 1991. 2d ed. *Human heredity: Principles and issues*. St. Paul, Minn.: West.

Darwin, C. 1839/1962. *The voyage of the Beagle*. New York: Anchor Books.

Davis, D. B. 1966/1969. A comparison of British America and Latin America. In L. Foner and E. D. Genovese, eds., *Slavery in the new world: A reader in comparative history*, 69–83. Englewood Cliffs, N.J.: Prentice-Hall.

Dawson, J. 1994. *Healing America's wounds*. Ventura, Calif.: Regal.

Dayton, D. W. 1975. From Christian perfection to the "Baptism of the Holy Ghost." In V. Synan, ed., *Aspects of Pentecostal-charismatic origins*, 39–54. Plainfield, New Jersey: Logos International.

Dean, M., et al. 1994. Polymorphic admixture typing in human ethnic populations. *Am. J. Hum. Genet.* 55:788–808.

DiLalla D. L., et al. 1996. Heritability of MMPI personality indicators of psychopathology in twins reared apart. *Journal of Abnormal Psychology* 105:491–99.

Dillon, M. L. 1990. *Slavery attacked: Southern slaves and their allies 1619–1865.* Baton Rouge: Louisiana State University Press.

Douglass, F. 1855/1969. *My bondage and my freedom.* New York: Dover.

Downey, D. B., and R. M. Hyser. 1991. *No crooked death: Coatesville, Pennsylvania, and the lynching of Zachariah Walker.* Urbana: University of Illinois Press.

D'Souza, D. 1995. *The end of racism:Principles for a multiracial society.* New York: Free Press.

Duster, T. 1990. *Backdoor to eugenics.* New York: Routledge.

———. 1993. Notes from his plenary address on social implications of new biomedical technologies. Conference on "Science, technology and the Christian faith, 26–29 July, Concordia College, Moorhead, Minnesota.

Edwards, J. D., Jr. 1996. Purging racism from Christianity. Grand Rapids, Mich.: Zondervan.

Edwards, T. M. 1998. Family reunion: The revelation about Thomas Jefferson's liaison spotlights a sensitive racial issue—passing for white. *Time,* 23 November, 85–86.

Enda, J. 1997. This time, schoolhouse door is open. *Philadelphia Inquirer,* 26 September, A1, A14.

Evans, A. T. 1995. *Let's get to know each other.* Nashville: Thomas Nelson.

Finney, C. G. n. d. (c. 1835)/1978. *Revivals of religion.* Virginia Beach, Va.: CBN University Press.

Flynn, J. R. 1998. IQ gains over time: toward finding the causes. In U. Neisser, ed., *The rising curve,* 25–66. Washington, D.C.: American Psychological Association.

Franco, M. H. L. P., T. A. Weimer, and F. M. Salzano. 1982. Blood polymorphisms and racial admixture in two Brazilian populations. *Amer. J. Phys. Anthropology* 58:127–32.

Frederickson, G. M. 1968. *William Lloyd Garrison.* Englewood Cliffs, N.J.: Prentice-Hall.

———. 1981. *White supremacy: A comparative study in American and*

South African history. New York: Oxford University Press.

Foster, E. A., et al. 1998. Jefferson fathered slave's last child. *Nature* 396:27–28.

Fox, P.W., et al. 1996. Genetic and environmental contributions to the acquisition of a motor skill. *Nature* 384:356–58.

Fyfe, C. 1994. Using race as an instrument of policy: A historical review. *Race and Class* 36:69–77.

Galen. 1968. *On the usefulness of the parts of the body.* Vol 2. Translated by M. Tallmadge. Ithaca, N.Y.: Cornell University Press.

Galton, F. 1869/1962. *Hereditary genius: An inquiry into its laws and consequences.* Cleveland: World.

Gardner, H. 1983. *Frames of mind: The theory of multiple intelligences.* New York: Basic.

Gelman, D., et al. 1992. Is this child gay? Born or bred? The origins of homosexuality. *Newsweek,* 24 February, 46–53.

Genovese, E. D. 1972. *Roll, Jordan, roll: The world the slaves made.* New York: Pantheon.

Gibbons, A. 1997. Y chromosome shows that Adam was African. *Science* 278: 804–5.

Gill, G. W. 1998. The beauty of race and races. *Anthropology Newsletter* 39(3):1, 4–5.

Goodman, P. 1998. *Of one blood: Abolitionism and the origins of racial equality.* Berkeley and Los Angeles: University of California Press.

Gould, S. J. 1981. *The mismeasure of man.* New York: Norton.

———. 1996. *The mismeasure of man, revised and expanded.* New York: Norton.

Grant, G. 1988. *Grand illusions: the legacy of Planned Parenthood.* Brentwood, Tennessee: Wolgemuth and Hyatt Publishers, Inc.

Greenfield, P. M. 1998. The cultural evolution of IQ. In U. Neisser, ed., *The rising curve,* 125–54. Washington, D.C.: American Psychological Association.

Grissmer, D. W., et al. 1998. Exploring the rapid rise in black achievement scores in the United States (1970–1990). In U. Neisser, ed., *The rising curve,* 251–68. Washington, D.C.: American Psychological Association.

Gutiérrez, G. 1992/1993. *Las Casas: In search of the poor of Jesus Christ.* Translated by R. R. Barr. Maryknoll, N.Y.: Orbis.

Hammer, M. F. 1995. A recent common ancestry for human Y chromosomes. *Nature* 378:376–78.

Hanke, L. 1959. *Aristotle and the American Indians: A study of race prejudice in the modern world.* Chicago: Henry Regnery.

Hamsitis, C. L., et al. 1991. Origins of U.S. Hispanics: implications for diabetes. *Diabetes Care 14* (Suppl. 3): 618–27.

Hauser, R. M. 1998. Trends in black-white test-score differentials: I. Uses and misuses of NAEP/SAT data. In U. Neisser, ed., *The rising curve,* 219–50. Washington, D.C.: American Psychological Association.

Helps, A. 1896/1970. *The life of Las Casas.* Williamstown, Mass.: John Lilburne.

Hemming, J. 1970. *The conquest of the Incas.* London: Papermac-Macmillan.

Herrnstein, R. J., and C. Murray. 1994. *The bell curve.* New York: Free Press.

Hodgen, M. T. 1964. *Early anthropology in the sixteenth and seventeenth centuries.* Philadelphia: University of Pennsylvania Press.

Holmes, S. J. 1936. *Human genetics and its social import.* New York: McGraw-Hill.

Hubbard, R. , and E. Wald. 1993. *Exploding the gene myth.* Boston: Beacon.

Human Genome Project. 1998. The official Internet information site as of 1999 was maintained by Oak Ridge National Laboratory at www.ornl.gov/hgmis

Infusino, D. 1995. Out of character: Nichelle Nichols. *TV Guide* "Collectors' Edition—Star Trek," 56.

Jacobs, H. A. 1861/1987. *Incidents in the life of slave girl, told by herself.* Cambridge, Mass.: Harvard University Press.

Kidd, K. K., et al. 1998. A global survey of haplotype frequencies and linkage disequilibrium at the DRD2 locus. *Human Genetics* 103:211–27.

King, M. L., Jr. 1963/1967. I have a dream. The complete text of the 28 August 1963 speech was obtained from J. H. Franklin and I. Starr, eds., *The Negro in twentieth-century America: A reader of the struggle for civil rights.* New York: Vintage.

Kingdom Identity Ministries. n.d. Doctrinal statement of beliefs. Downloaded in autumn 1998 from www.kingidentity.com

Kizilos, P. J. 1983. Dight Institute benefactor advocated eugenics. *Minnesota Daily,* July 13, 1, 5.

Kottak, C. P. 1994. 6th ed. *Cultural anthropology.* New York: McGraw-Hill.

Las Casas, B. 1552/1970. *Tears of the Indians.* Translated by J. Phillips (1656). Williamstown, Mass.: John Lilburne.

LaVey, S. 1991. A difference in the hypothalamic structure between hetere-osexual and homosexual men. *Science* 253:1034–37.

Lefkowitz, M. 1996. *Not out of Africa: How Afrocentrism became an excuse to teach myth as history.* New York: Basic.

Lessner, L. 1999. The writer who inspired suspects in hate crimes. *Philadelphia Inquirer,* August 17, A1, A8.

Lewis, B. 1990. *Race and slavery in the Middle East.* Oxford: Oxford University Press.

Lewis, J., and M. D'Orso. *Walking with the wind: A memoir of the movement.* New York: Simon and Schuster.

Lewthwaite, G. A., and G. Kane. 1996. Where children live in bondage; Inquiry: is there slavery in Sudan? Louis Farrakhan, a friend of the regime scoffs. To find out, two Sun reporters make an illegal journey to see—and experience—a monstrous truth. This is their journal. *Baltimore Sun,* 16 June, 1A. Full text available on-line via www.sunspot.net

Lewthwaite, G. A., and G. Kane. 1996. Horror in villages haunted by slavery. *Baltimore Sun,* 17 June, 1A. Full text available on-line via www.sunspot.net

Lewthwaite, G. A., and G. Kane. 1996. Bought—and freed; Freedom: for a handful of cash, our reporters strike a deal with an Arab middleman, freeing two young boys after six years of bondage. The exchange proves beyond all doubt that slavery exists in Sudan. *Baltimore Sun,* 18 June, p. Full text available on-line via www.sunspot.net

Long, J. C., et al. 1991. Genetic variaion in Arizona Mexican Americans: Estimation and interpretation of admixture proportions. *Amer. J. Phys. Anthropology* 84:141–57.

Lovett, L. 1975. Black Origins of the Pentecostal movement. In V. Synan, ed., *Aspects of Pentecostal-charismatic origins,* 123–142. Plainfield, New Jersey: Logos International.

Lykken, D. T., et al. 1992. Emergenesis: genetic traits that may not run in families. *American Psychologist* 47:1565–77.

Lynn, R. 1998. In support of the nutrition theory. In U. Neisser, ed., *The rising curve,* 207–18. Washington, D.C.: American Psychological Association.

Magnuson, N. 1977. *Salvation in the slums: Evangelical social work, 1865–1920.* Grand Rapids, Mich.: Baker.

Marshall, R. G. and C. A. Donovan. 1991. *Blessed are the barren: the social policy of Planned Parenthood.* San Francisco: Ignatius Press.

Martorell, R. 1998. Nutrition and the worldwide rise in IQ scores. In U. Neisser, ed., *The rising curve,* 183–206. Washington, D.C.: American Psychological Association.

Mieses, I. 1998. Ni negros, ni mulatos, ni blancos . . . dominicanos. *Listín Diario* (Santo Domingo, Dominican Republic), 11 October, 16–17.

Mountain, J. L., and L. L. Cavalli-Sforza. 1997. Multilocus genotypes, a tree of individuals, and human evolutionary history. *Amer. J. Hum. Genetics* 61:705–18.

Murray, B., and B. Duffy. 1998. Jefferson's secret life. *U. S. News and World Report,* November 9, 59–63.

Myers, B. L. 1999. *Walking with the poor: Principles and practice of transformational development.* Maryknoll, N.Y.: Orbis.

Ogbu, J. U. 1988. Human intelligence testing: a cultural-ecological perspective. *National Forum: the Phi Kappa Phi Journal* 68:23–29.

Olby, R. C. 1966. *Origins of Mendelism.* New York: Schocken.

Ortíz de Montellano, B. R. 1993. Melanin, Afrocentricity and pseudoscience. *Yearbook of Physical Anthropology* 36:33–58.

PBS. 1998. What happened in South Africa? Reports that the apartheid regime used biological weapons. In *Frontline: Plague War.* Available on the internet at http://cgi.pbs.org/wgbh/pages/frontline/show/plague.

Perkins, J. M. 1976. *Let justice roll down.* Glendale, Calif.: Regal.

———. 1982. *With justice for all.* Ventura, Calif.: Regal.

Perkins, S., and C. Rice. 1993. *More than equals: Racial healing for the sake of the gospel.* Downers Grove, Ill.: InterVarsity Press.

Plato. 1985. *The Republic.* Translated by R. W. Sterling and W. C. Scott. New York: Norton.

Plomin, R. 1990. The role of inheritance in behavior. *Science* 248:183–88.

Poponoe, P., and Johnson, R. H. 1920. *Applied eugenics.* New York: Macmillan.

Prosper of Aquitaine. c. 450/1952. *The call of all nations.* Translated by P. De Letter. Westminster, Md.: Newman Press.

Relethford, J. H. 1998. Genetics of modern human origins and diversity. *Annual Review of Anthropology* 27:1–23.

Reuters. 1998. Sudáfrica buscó bacteria para eliminar a los negros o esterilizarlos. *El comercio* (Lima, Peru), 13 June, B1.

Samuel, T. 1994. Bell curve trail leads to an outfit with a racial bent. *Philadelphia Inquirer,* 27 November, E3.

Shirer, W. 1959, 1960. *The rise and fall of the Third Reich.* New York: Simon & Schuster.

Shurkin, J. N. 1992. *Terman's kids.* Boston: Little, Brown.

Sigman, M., and S. E. Whaley. 1998. The role of nutrition in the development of intelligence. In U. Neisser, ed., *The rising curve,* 155–82. Washington, D.C.: American Psychological Association.

Sinclair, U. 1906/1965. *The jungle.* New York: Heritage Press.

Spurdle, A. B., and T. Jenkins. 1996. The origins of the Lemba "Black Jews" of southern Africa: evidence from p12F2 and other Y-chromosome markers. *Am. J. Hum. Genet.* 59:1126–33.

Stern, C. 1970. Model estimates of the number of gene pairs involved in pigmentation variability of the Negro-American. *Human Heredity* 20:165–68.

Still, W. 1871/1970. *The Underground Railroad.* Chicago: Ebony Classics, Johnson Publishing.

Stringer, C., and McKie, R. 1997. *African exodus: The origins of modern humanity.* New York: Holt.

Tannenbaum, F. 1963/1969. Slavery, the Negro and racial prejudice. In L. Foner and E. D. Genovese, eds., *Slavery in the new world: A reader in comparative history,* 3–7. Englewood Cliffs, N. J.: Prentice-Hall.

Terman, L. M. et al., eds. 1925/renewed 1959. Genetic studies of genius. Vol. 1: *Mental and physical traits of a thousand gifted children.* Stanford, Calif.: Stanford University Press.

Tishkoff, S. A., et al. 1996. Global patterns of linkage disequilibrium at the CD4 locus and modern human origins. *Science* 271:1380–87.

Tournier, P. 1977/1978. *The violence within.* Translated by E. Hudson. San Francisco: Harper and Row.

Weary, D., and W. Hendricks. 1990. *I ain't comin' back.* Wheaton, Ill.: Tyndale House.

Weatherford, J. 1988. *Indian givers: How the Indians of the Americas transformed the world.* New York: Fawcett Columbine.

Wesley, J. Various dates/1938. *The journal of John Wesley.* Edited by A.M. N. Curnock. London: Epworth. Quotes were taken from volumes 5, 7, and 8.

Wesley, J. 1774. *Thoughts upon slavery.* Philadelphia: Joseph Cruikshank.

Williams, E. 1944/1966. *Capitalism and slavery.* New York: Capricorn Books, G. P. Putnam's Sons.

Whitfield, L. S., et al. 1995. Sequence variation of the human Y chromosome. *Nature* 378:379–80.

Woolman, J. 1774/1952. *The journal and other writings.* New York: E. P. Dutton.

Young, B. 1865. *The laws of God relative to the African race: Journal of discourses.* 10:110. Liverpool: Daniel H. Wells.

Zietkiewicz, E., et al. 1997. Nuclear DNA diversity in worldwide distributed human population. *Gene* 205:161–71.

Zietkiewicz, E., et al. 1998. Genetic structure of the ancestral populations of modern humans. *J. Molecular Evolution* 47:146–55.

Zimmerman, T. F. 1975. The reason for the rise of the Pentecostal movement. In V. Synan, ed., *Aspects of Pentecostal-charismatic origins,* 5–14. Plainfield, N.J.: Logos International.